MEDICAL MALPRACTICE:

STRATEGIC AND PRACTICAL PRINCIPLES

Library of Congress Catalog Card Number: 85-61222
ISBN Number: 0-942954-08-4

MEDICAL MALPRACTICE: STRATEGIC AND PRACTICAL PRINCIPLES

Editor-in-Chief

Robert Devine

Contributing Authors

Emmet J. Agoglia, Esq.
Kathleen M. Beckett, Esq.
Richard Coburn, M. D.
Ira A. Cohen, Esq.
Joseph M. Costello, Esq.
Peter C. Kopff, Esq.
Stanley A. Landers, Esq.
Harry H. Lipsig, Esq.
John P. LoPresti, Jr., Esq.
John R. Marshall, Jr., Esq.
Steven E. Pegalis, Esq.
Fred Peters, Esq.
Luke M. Pittoni, Esq.
Thomas J. Principe, Esq.
Herman Schmertz, Esq.
Arthur N. Seiff, Esq.
Richard E. Shandell, Esq.
Henry R. Simon, R.Ph., J. D.
Andrew Sulner, M. S., J. D.
Harvey F. Wachsman, M. D., J. D.
Harvey Weitz, Esq.
Ernest F. W. Wildermuth, Jr., Esq.
Hon. Fred T. Santucci

New York State Bar Association®

1986

NYSBA

DEDICATION

This book is dedicated to the memory of Fred Peters, a lawyer who had so much—and was willing to share it.

FOREWORD

In offering this book, *Medical Malpractice: Strategic and Practical Principles,* to the legal profession, the New York State Bar Association has called upon the expertise of our State's most experienced trial lawyers in the field to author the informative articles contained therein. The result is a work that promises pleasure and profit to the members of the legal profession from the mere perusal of its chapters.

The contributing lawyers hold enviable positions as leaders of the New York Trial bar, and their articles illustrate their own precepts and experiences. Besides offering basic legal principles governing medical malpractice actions, the book is enriched by substantial discussions of the theory and strategy utilized in the preparation and defense of a medical malpractice case.

The book is packed with wisdom and knowledge beneficial not only to the neophyte medical malpractice attorney, but also to the most experienced tactician and strategist. Substantively, the work provides a comprehensive overview of medical malpractice topics, including the most powerful weapon in the legal armory, the examination before trial of the plaintiff and of the defendant physician; the medical malpractice panel hearing; the jury selection process or *voir dire* (from both plaintiff's and defendant's perspectives); the presentation of medical proof; the use of legal texts and treatises; special areas of consideration, such as drugs in medical malpractice litigation; obtaining, as well as the presentation and use of, an expert witness for trial, and, most important for trial lawyers, the requests to charge from the vantage of both plaintiffs and defendants. These, then, are just some examples of the breadth of the articles contributed by the experienced trial advocates.

Every lawyer familiar with the litigation process has seen medical malpractice cases won by thorough preparation, or lost by inadequate preparation of trial counsel. It is true that only experience can develop the skills of a successful advocate, but to say that only practice can breed perfection is not to deny the value of precept and example. These the contributors of this book relate in their most palatable form. Young attorneys and veterans of the bar alike will profit by reading what these experienced advocates have laid before them.

Seymour Boyers
Former Associate Justice of the
Appellate Division
State of New York
Second Judicial Department

TABLE OF CONTENTS

DETAILED TABLE OF CONTENTS

CHAPTER ONE

BASIC LEGAL PRINCIPLES GOVERNING MEDICAL MALPRACTICE ACTIONS

Arthur N. Seiff, Esq.

I. SUBJECT MATTER COVERED BY THIS ARTICLE

The intent of this article is to call attention to some basic areas of substantive and procedural law governing medical malpractice actions which, on being overlooked during trial, have been grounds for appellate intervention with resultant loss of a hard fought for and apparently won verdict. Because the prime end of trial counsel (both those representing plaintiffs and those representing defendants) should be to achieve a favorable result which will withstand appellate scrutiny, all trial counsel, plaintiffs' and defendants', should bear these areas in mind in both preparing for trial and trying their cases.

Obviously, the limited length of an article such as this prevents the inclusion of all (or even a major part of) the substantive and procedural law aspects involved in such a case.

II. NATURE OF ACTION AND BURDEN OF PROOF

Generically, a medical malpractice action is based on negligence. *Cubito v. Kreisberg*, 69 A.D.2d 738, 742 (2d Dep't 1979), *aff'd*, 51 N.Y.2d 900 (1980). Understandably, the standard of care required of a physician is that of a reasonably prudent physician. *Sanabria v. City of New York*, 42 A.D.2d 615 (2d Dep't 1973).

As in other actions based on a defendant's alleged negligence, a plaintiff in a medical malpractice action (1) has the burden of establishing affirmatively that there was a malpractice on the part of defendant and (2) must also establish that the defendant's malpractice was a proximate cause of the alleged injury. Where plaintiff fails to prove proximate causation, the courts have consistently dismissed the complaint or directed a verdict for defendant despite the presence of evidence of malpractice. *Foley v. Gillick*, 39 A.D.2d 546 (2d Dep't 1972); *Vara v. Drago*, 24 A.D.2d 888 (2d Dep't 1965); *Quinones v. St. Vincent's Hospital*, 20 A.D.2d 529 (1st Dep't 1963), *aff'd*, 16 N.Y.2d 572 (1965); *Greenberg v. Jewish Hospital of Brooklyn*, 43 A.D.2d 664 (1973); *Garzione v. Vassar Brothers Hospital*, 36 A.D.2d 390 (1st Dep't 1971), *aff'd*, 30 N.Y.2d 857 (1972).

III. DUTY OWED BY PHYSICIAN

Liability of a defendant founded in negligence is based on an alleged breach of duty by the defendant. *Pulka v. Edelman*, 40 N.Y.2d 781, 782 (1976). A physician, in treating a patient, has three component duties, (1) "to possess the requisite knowledge and skill such as is possessed by the average member of the medical possession" [*sic*, obviously meant to be profession], (2) "to exercise ordinary and reasonable care in the application of such professional knowledge and skill," and (3) "to use his best judgment in the application of this knowledge and skill." *Littlejohn v. State of New York*, 87 A.D.2d 951, 952 (3d Dep't 1982). To this must be added, as stated by the Court of Appeals, "that a physician should [also use] whatever superior knowledge, skill and intelligence he has," and thus a specialist may be liable in a situation in which a general practitioner would not be liable. *Toth v. Community Hospital at Glen Cove*, 22 N.Y.2d 255, 262-263 (1968).

A mistake in judgment does not of itself render a physician liable. Where the physician has acted in the exercise of his judgment, he is exonerated from liability even if it develops that he was wrong and that injury was caused to plaintiff thereby. *Pigno v. Bunim*, 43 A.D.2d 718 (2d Dep't 1973), *aff'd*, 35 N.Y.2d 841 (1974); *Bullock v. Parkchester General Hospital*, 3 A.D.2d 254, 257 (1st Dep't 1957), *aff'd*, 4 N.Y.2d 894 (1958); *Centeno v. City of New York*, 48 A.D.2d 812, 813 (1st Dep't 1975), *aff'd*, 40 N.Y.2d 932 (1976); *Davis v. State of New York*, 35 A.D.2d 762, 763 (3d Dep't 1970). The Court of Appeals noted that "The art of healing frequently calls for a balancing of risks and dangers to a patient." *Perlmutter v. Beth David Hospital*, 308 N.Y. 100, 107 (1954).

There are many cases, decided on the basis of this principle, in which the physician has been exonerated of liability as a matter of law. Under this doctrine, an action was dismissed where there was a wrong diagnosis, *Rosario v. State of New York*, 33 A.D.2d 122 (3d Dep't 1969), *aff'd*, 36 N.Y.2d 901 (1975), where there was a wrong prognosis, *Centeno v. City of New York*, 48 A.D.2d 812 (1st Dep't 1975), *aff'd*, 40 N.Y.2d 932 (1976), *Taig v. State of New York*, 19 A.D.2d 182 (3d Dep't 1963), where there was an error in medical judgment, *Davis v. State of New York*, 35 A.D.2d 762, 763 (3d Dep't 1970), where a diagnosis and decision were wrong, *Cameron v. State of New York*, 37 A.D.2d 46, *aff'd*, 30 N.Y.2d 596 (1972), where there was a disagreement between experts and the defendant's opinion was an honest one, *Centeno, supra*.

A caveat is that the exercise of judgment by the physician presupposes that he undertook to obtain sufficient information to make a medical judgment, that he made a careful and competent examination and that he performed required tests: a failure to do so would be a failure to exercise any judgment for which he would be held liable. *Bell v. New York City Health & Hospitals Corp.*, 90 A.D.2d 270, 280-282 (2d Dep't 1982); *Lipsius v. White*, 91 A.D.2d 271, 277 (2d Dep't 1983); *Pigno v. Bunim*, 43 A.D.2d 718, *aff'd*, 35 N.Y.2d 841 (1974); *Plumadore v. State of New York*, 75 A.D.2d 691, 692 (3d Dep't 1980).

Because it is recognized that "[m]edicine is not an exact science," where there is a difference of opinion as to what should be done in a given situation, a physician may "elect which method to use." *Gielski v. State of New York*, 10 A.D.2d 471, 473 (3d Dep't 1960), *aff'd*, 9 N.Y.2d 834 (1961). Accordingly, even if his judgment was a mistaken judgment, a physician will not be held liable for having adopted the procedure he did adopt in a situation in which it was a matter of professional medical judgment as to whether he should or should not follow that particular procedure. *Pike v. Honsinger*, 155 N.Y. 201, 210 (1898); *Pigno v. Bunim*, 43 A.D.2d 718 (2d Dep't 1973), *aff'd*, 35 N.Y.2d 841 (1974); *Bullock v. Parkchester General Hospital*, 3 A.D.2d 254 (1st Dep't 1957), *aff'd*, 4 N.Y.2d 894 (1958); *St. George v. State of New York*, 283 A.D. 245, 248 (1954), *aff'd*, 308 N.Y. 681 (1954); *Centeno v. City of New York*, 48 A.D.2d 812, 813 (1st Dep't 1975), *aff'd*, 40 N.Y.2d 932 (1976); *Davis v. State of New York*, 35 A.D.2d 762, 763 (3d Dep't 1972). This principle is stated succinctly in *Schreiber v. Cestari*, 40 A.D.2d 1025, 1026 (2d Dep't 1972): "Where alternative procedures are available to a physician, any one of which is medically acceptable and proper under the circumstances, a physician cannot be held liable for malpractice when he uses one of two acceptable techniques."

In *Toth v. Community Hospital at Glen Cove*, 22 N.Y.2d 255, 263 (1968), the Court of Appeals gave the underlying reason for this: "Fairness and the avoidance of any principle of strict liability would seem to require that the physician not be held liable for exercising his best judgment at least in the case where the procedures used by the physician had some reputable support in the profession."

IV. EFFECT OF STANDARDS OF PRACTICE ADOPTED BY THE MEDICAL PROFESSION

Applicable to negligence actions generally is the rule that: (1) complying with a standard or custom is evidence of care but does not preclude a finding that there was negligence, *Saglimbeni v. West End Brewing Co.*, 274 A.D. 201 (1948), *aff'd*, 298 N.Y. 875 (1949); *T. J. Hooper*, 60 F.2d 737 (1932); *Prosser, Torts*, 4th ed., 33; *Phillips v. Roux Laboratories*, 286 A.D. 549 (1955); *Trimarco v. Klein*, 56 N.Y.2d 98, 105-106 (1982); *Miner v. Long Island Lighting Co.*, 40 N.Y.2d 372, 381 (1976); *Sherman v. M. Lowenstein & Sons, Inc.*, 28 A.D.2d 922 (2d Dep't 1967); *Storm v. N.Y. Tel. Co.*, 270 N.Y. 103 (1936); *Garthe v. Ruppert*, 264 N.Y. 290 (1934); and (2) failing to comply with the standard or custom is evidence that there was negligence, *Trimarco, supra*; *Phillips, supra*; *Miner, supra*; *Sherman, supra*. But, the courts have held that ultimately it is a question for the courts to decide whether there was care and that the calling or industry cannot set a controlling standard. *The T. J. Hooper*, 60 F.2d 737 (1932); *Trimarco v. Klein*, 56 N.Y.2d 98, 105-106 (1982).

It should be noted that a self-imposed custom and practice, imposed by the particular defendant on himself, is to be taken into consideration. *Cappel v. Board of Education*, 40 A.D.2d 848 (2d Dep't 1972); *Dolan v. H. C. Bohack, Inc.*, 35 A.D.2d 672 (2d Dep't 1970). This rule is applicable to the medical profession.

The Court of Appeals has held that "[t]he law generally permits the medical profession to establish its own standard of care" and that "evidence that a physician conformed to accepted community standards of practice usually insulates him from tort liability." *Toth v. Community Hospital at Glen Cove*, 22 N.Y.2d 255, 262 (1968).

It also has held that "evidence that the defendant followed customary practice is not the sole test of professional malpractice," that "[i]f a physician fails to employ his expertise or best judgment, and that omission causes injury, he should not automatically be freed from liability because in fact he adhered to acceptable practice." *Toth v. Community Hospital at Glen Cove*, 22 N.Y.2d 255, 262-263 (1968); *Burton v. Brooklyn Doctors Hospital*, 88 A.D.2d 217 (1st Dep't 1982).

The above rule and qualification to that rule are implicit in the statement of the Court of Appeals in *Toth* that the law "generally" permits the medical profession to establish its own standard of care and that a physician who conforms thereto is "usually" insulated from tort liability. 22 N.Y.2d at 262.

V. REGARDING PROOF THAT A BAD RESULT FOLLOWED THE TREATMENT OR THE OPERATION

The average layperson, and too many attorneys, have the impression that the fact that there was a bad result following the physician's treatment or the surgeon's operation is evidence of fault, i.e., malpractice, in the treatment or operation. Such an impression, followed by reliance thereon, has proved the Achilles' heel of many cases. Directly contrary to the above impression, it is well-established that the failure of treatment or the failure of an operation or the occurrence of a bad result does not of itself permit an inference that there was malpractice. *Henry v. Bronx Lebanon Medical Center*, 53 A.D.2d 476, 480 (1st Dep't 1976); *Robbins v. Nathan*, 189 A.D. 827, 828-829 (1919); *McDermott v. Manhattan Eye, Ear & Throat Hospital*, 16 A.D.2d 374 (1st Dep't 1962), *aff'd*, 15 N.Y.2d 20, 24 (1964); *Filanowicz v. Guarino*, 27 A.D.2d 666 (2d Dep't 1967) *mod.*; *Zeleznik v. Jewish Chronic Disease Hospital*, 47 A.D.2d 199 (2d Dep't 1966). This was stated succinctly in *Henry, supra*: "Presence of an injury does not mean that there was negligence."

The Court of Appeals has stated that to hold that a bad result which causes an injury is proof of negligence would be to make the doctor a guarantor, which is impermissible. *Pike v. Honsinger*, 155 N.Y. 201, 210 (1898).

VI. REGARDING *RES IPSA LOQUITUR*

Res ipsa loquitur has been held to be applicable to a medical malpractice action in situations in which (1) "the injury occurred outside the site of an operation," or (2) "where a foreign object is left within the body of a patient after an operation" or (3) where "the injury occurred while the patient was under an anesthesia." *Pipers v. Rosenow*, 39 A.D.2d 240, 243 (2d Dep't 1972); *Matlick v. Long Island Jewish Hospital*, 25 A.D.2d 538, 539 (2d Dep't 1966); *Fogal v. Genesee Hospital*, 41 A.D.2d 468, 475 (4th Dep't 1973).

Generally, a plaintiff's attorney should be hesitant about relying solely on the theory of *res ipsa loquitur.* Unless, of course, there is no other way available to him in which he can establish a cause of action. In many instances, reliance on that doctrine has led to dismissal of the action. For example, the *Pipers* case, *supra*, from which the above quotations were taken, held that "an injury to a nerve following the use of a needle for the withdrawal of blood" does not constitute *res ipsa loquitur,* even though it was also proved that "blood was drawn on the first occasion [that the needle was used] without any negative result" and that the injury came on the second occasion the needle was used. In *George v. City of New York*, 22 A.D.2d 70 (1st Dep't 1964), *aff'd*, 17 N.Y.2d 561 (1966), the perforation of a wall of the bowel in the course of the administration of a barium enema was held not to invoke *res ipsa loquitur.* The danger of a plaintiff's reliance on *res ipsa loquitur* is demonstrated by the fact that in *George,* plaintiff recovered a judgment on the basis of a jury verdict but the Appellate Division reversed that judgment and dismissed the plaintiff's complaint and the Court of Appeals affirmed the dismissal of the complaint.

There are many more adjudications which demonstrate the inherent danger in the seemingly inviting doctrine of *res ipsa loquitur.*

VII. THE NEED FOR EXPERT TESTIMONY

It is advisable, and in most cases indispensable, that plaintiff produce expert testimony to establish a cause of action. To try a case without expert testimony is to risk dismissal as a matter of law. The absence of expert testimony has frequently been held fatal to plaintiff's action. *Robbins v. Nathan*, 189 A.D. 827, 830 (1919); *Morgan v. State*, 40 A.D.2d 891 (3d Dep't 1972), *aff'd*, 34 N.Y.2d 709 (1974); *Spitzer v. Ciprut*, 80 A.D.2d 891 (2d Dep't 1981); *Morwin v. Albany Hospital*, 7 A.D.2d 582, 584 (3d Dep't 1959); *Tobias v. Manhattan Eye, Ear & Throat Hospital*, 28 A.D.2d 972, *aff'd*, 23 N.Y.2d 724 (1968); *Pipers v. Rosenow*, 39 A.D.2d 240, 243 (2d Dep't 1972); *Cassano v. Hagstrom*, 5 N.Y.2d 643, 646 (1959); *Charlton v. Montefiore Hospital*, 45 Misc. 2d 153, 157 (1965).

In *Robbins*, *supra*, the Court stated:

> If the treatment of the defendant was unskillful or negligent, it was incumbent upon the plaintiff to show it by those qualified to

> testify to the proper method of performing such an operation; and if the untoward results present here might have been avoided by due care, the duty of showing that was also on the plaintiff.

In *Tobias*, *supra*, the Court (1) reversed a judgment for plaintiff and (2) dismissed plaintiff's complaint because of "the absence of medical proof. . . that the defendants' acts were not in accordance with accepted medical practice" and thus, stated the Court, there was "no legal basis for the judgment."

This applies both to proof of malpractice and to proof of proximate causation, an additional requirement in a medical malpractice action, as it is in other actions based on negligence. *Charlton v. Montefiore Hospital*, 45 Misc. 2d 153 (1965); *McDermott v. Manhattan Eye, Ear & Throat Hospital*, 15 N.Y.2d 20, 24 (1964); *Filanowicz v. Guarino*, 27 A.D.2d 666 (2d Dep't 1967); *Meiselman v. Crown Heights Hospital*, 285 N.Y. 389 (1941); *Zeleznik v. Jewish Chronic Disease Hospital*, 47 A.D.2d 199 (2d Dep't 1975).

The reason for this was stated in *Pipers*, *supra*:

> . . . the science of medicine is recondite; and, in the ordinary case of malpractice, a jury is not equipped to determine the issue of negligence simply as an inference from the circumstances * * * The information obtained from an expert witness supplies the jury with the means by which it can evaluate the conduct of the party charged with malpractice.

Just as the trier of the facts (be it jury or be it judge) will not be permitted to infer malpractice from the occurrence of a bad result, so also an expert witness will not be permitted to assume or to testify that there was negligence on the basis of the fact that there was a bad result. *McDermott v. Manhattan Eye, Ear & Throat Hospital*, 26 A.D.2d 519 (1st Dep't 1966), *aff'd*, 18 N.Y.2d 970 (1966); *Dembicer v. Rosenthal*, 53 Misc. 2d 777 (1962), *aff'd*, 20 A.D.2d 758 (1964); *Holzberg v. Flower and Fifth Avenue Hospital*, 39 A.D.2d 526 (1st Dep't 1972), *aff'd*, 32 N.Y.2d 716 (1973); *Cassano v. Hagstrom*, 5 N.Y.2d 643, 645 (1959).

VIII. REGARDING EXPERT TESTIMONY

As regards the "expert" to be produced, it should be remembered that there is a distinction between an expert and a knowledgeable person. *Kulak v. Na-*

tionwide Insurance Co., 40 N.Y.2d 140 (1976). It has been held that whether the witness is an expert is subject to the discretion of the trial court in assessing his qualifications. *National Conversion Corp. v. Cedar Bldg. Corp.*, 23 N.Y.2d 621 (1969); *Molinari v. Conforti v. Eisele, Inc.*, 54 A.D.2d 1113 (4th Dep't 1976). It has also been held that a licensed doctor may testify as an expert in any field of medicine, even though he is not a specialist in that field, *Kletnieks v. Brookhaven Mem. Assn.*, 53 A.D.2d 169, 175 (2d Dep't 1976); *Fuller v. Preis*, 35 N.Y.2d 425 (1974); *Harris v. Smith*, 372 F.2d 806 (1967), and that even a properly qualified person may testify although unlicensed to practice medicine, *Badke v. Barnett*, 35 A.D.2d 347, 349 (2d Dep't 1970), *appeal denied*, 28 N.Y.2d 482 (1970).

There is no ritualistic formula to which the expression of an expert's opinion must conform. The probative force of testimony by "non-lawyer witnesses" will not be defeated by semantics or because they "fail to use the words preferred by lawyers and Judges." *Ward v. Kovacs*, 55 A.D.2d 391, 397 (2d Dep't 1977). Contrary to the general impression, an expert's use of the words "possible," "potential," "I think," "apparently," and even "I would not swear to it," does not invalidate his testimony. *Spadaccini v. Dolan*, 63 A.D.2d 110, 115 (1st Dep't 1978); *Reich v. Evans*, 7 A.D.2d 765 (3d Dep't 1958); *Blake v. People*, 73 N.Y. 586 (1878); *People v. Daghita*, 276 A.D. 20 (1949), *modified on other grounds*, 310 N.Y. 223 (1950); *Hallahan v. N.Y.L.E. and W.R.R.*, 102 N.Y. 194 (1886). What the courts look for is the thought and meaning. They do not require testimony in terms of certainty or infallibility. *Ernest v. Boggs Lake Estate*, 12 N.Y.2d 414, 415 (1963).

Both plaintiffs' and defendants' trial counsel should note that the fact that an expert during his direct examination has rendered an opinion favorable to the party calling him, that does not always save the party from the danger of an appellate court holding that the expert's direct testimony was destroyed *as a matter of law* by cross-examination. This, despite the general rule that the credibility of a witness who has given unfavorable or contradictory testimony presents a question of fact for the jury. *Spampinato v. A.B.C. Constr. Corp.*, 35 N.Y.2d 283 (1974); *People v. Reed*, 40 N.Y.2d 204, 207 (1976). The general rule was applied to the testimony of an expert whose testimony on cross-examination refuted his testimony on direct examination. *Board of Education v. Hueber*, 90 A.D.2d 685 (4th Dep't 1982).

The danger stems from a statement by the Court of Appeals in *Miller v. National Cabinet Co.*, 8 N.Y.2d 277, 283 (1960), that the doctor's testimony on direct examination "loses 'all probative force when supplemented and explained' by the testimony which he gave upon cross-examination."

Although the trier of facts is not bound by the opinion of an expert witness, *Felt v. Olson*, 51 N.Y.2d 977, 979 (1980), if the trier of facts rejects an expert's opinion and reaches a contrary conclusion, there must exist an independent basis in the record to support such contrary conclusion. *In re City of New York (A. & W. Realty Corp.)*, 1 N.Y.2d 428, 432-433 (1956).

IX. REGARDING HOSPITALS

Rules applicable to physicians are also applicable to hospitals. As to the latter, it should be noted that the hospital is not liable for the conduct of the injured person's own physician (who is called an attending). It is not uncommon for an attending physician to be held liable while the hospital where the patient was treated by that attending is exonerated. Since the attending (plaintiff's private physician) is an independent contractor rather than an employee of the hospital, a finding of malpractice by plaintiff's private doctor does not render the hospital liable. *Pigno v. Bunim*, 43 A.D.2d 718, *aff'd*, 35 N.Y.2d 841 (1974); *Toth v. Community Hospital at Glen Cove*, 22 N.Y.2d 255 (1968); *Fiorentino v. Wenger*, 19 N.Y.2d 407 (1967); *Garzione v. Vassar Brothers Hospital*, 36 A.D.2d 390, *aff'd*, 30 N.Y.2d 857 (1971).

On the other hand, where it is the hospital which supplies a physician to treat a patient who comes to the hospital for treatment, the hospital is liable to the patient for malpractice on the part of that physician despite the fact that that physician is an independent contractor. *Mduba v. Benedictine Hospital*, 52 A.D.2d 450 (3rd Dep't 1976).

Where the malpractice is that of an attending, i.e., the patient's private physician who is treating him in the hospital: (1) the hospital is not liable when its staff obeys the attending's orders; and (2) is liable when they do not. As was stated in *Toth*, *supra*, "They may not invade the area of the physician's competence and authority to overrule his orders," *Toth v. Community Hospital at Glen Cove*, 22 N.Y.2d, 255, 264-265; *accord Bamert v. Central General Hospital*, 53 N.Y.2d 656 (1981).

Toth noted an exception to the rule that the hospital is not liable where the hospital's staff obeys the plaintiff's private physician's orders, 22 N.Y.2d, *id.* at 265n: "An exception to the rule would exist where the hospital staff knows that the doctor's orders are so clearly contraindicated by normal practice that ordinary prudence requires inquiry into the correctness of the orders."

The other side of the coin is that it is the duty of the attending physician (1) to give proper instructions to the members of the hospital staff who are to take care of the patient and (2) to see to it that his orders are carried out. *Lium v. Ploski*, 87 A.D.2d 860 (2nd Dep't 1982).

X. CONTRIBUTORY NEGLIGENCE

Questions formerly were presented as to (1) the kind of contributory negligence and (2) when that contributory negligence happened, that would bar a plaintiff entirely from recovering a verdict. *Ferrara v. Leventhal*, 56 A.D.2d 490, 495-497 (2nd Dep't 1977); *Morse v. Rapkin*, 24 A.D.2d 24 (1st Dep't 1975); *Yardeny v. Fondacaro*, 57 A.D.2d 924 (2nd Dep't 1977); *Heller v. Medine*, 50 A.D.2d 831 (2nd Dep't 1975); *Quinones v. Public Administrator*, 49 A.D.2d 889 (1975); 45 New York Jurisprudence, *Physicians and Surgeons*, Section 171. Those questions have been made irrelevant by CPLR sec. 1411, the comparative negligence statute which now makes the question of a plaintiff's contributory negligence apply only to mitigation of plaintiff's damages. What remains is that contributory negligence goes to mitigation of plaintiff's damages. CPLR sec. 1411.

XI. FINAL CAVEAT

Many of the foregoing rules have ramifications and variations, the resolution of which depends on the particular facts of the case on trial. What has been attempted here has been to give an idea of some of the areas where problems usually will be encountered. It cannot be recommended too strongly that each case should be dealt with in the light of the precise facts in that particular case.

CHAPTER TWO

THE ROLE OF THE FORENSIC DOCUMENT EXAMINER IN MEDICAL MALPRACTICE CASES

Andrew Sulner, M.S., J.D.

I. INTRODUCTION

Despite the fact that one of the most common forms of evidence presented in court is documentary evidence, countless lawsuits are unnecessarily lost as a result of the attorney's acceptance of the adversary's documents at face value. Virtually all lawyers experienced in the trial of medical malpractice cases will not hesitate to agree that such lawsuits are generally won or lost on the medical records. Nevertheless, all too frequently, lawyers handling such cases fail to consider the possibility that the medical and/or hospital records involved in the case, as well as other types of documents offered as proof, may be spurious. The purpose of this article is to alert plaintiff and defense attorneys alike of the importance of approaching each set of medical records with a suspicious eye and to illustrate how the forensic document examiner can be utilized as a vital means of courtroom proof.

Although hospital accreditation requirements have established certain standards for record-keeping and supervision of patients' charts, the burden of satisfying these requirements and the demands placed upon the medical profession and hospital staff often contribute to departures from the routine record-keeping procedures. Thus, *post facto* changes or entries in a record can often be attributable to a customary and necessary delay in the recordation process rather than to fraudulent alterations and additions. For example, the post-operative Doctor's Progress Notes and the Nurse's Notes may contain several sequential entries written at one and the same time even though they pertain to events which may have transpired over several hours. Similarly, the Anesthesia Record and the Operative Record may have been prepared well after the operation was completed. In such cases, the medical significance of the detected irregularity in the record and the manner in which it was effectuated invariably establishes whether it was an innocent departure from customary record-keeping procedures or a wilful departure motivated by self-serving interests.

This article will use the case history format to illustrate instances of forged, altered and substituted medical records that have been discovered in the course of the author's professional practice. The cases selected are intended to provide the reader with a representative sample of the most common types of irregularities found in medical records and which every lawyer should be conscious of when evaluating a given case. The limited length of an article such as this necessarily precludes an extensive coverage of the subject matter.

The bulk of documentary medical evidence consists of hospital records and physician's office records. The attorney's inquiries with respect to such records are usually limited to a few key entries on particular dates, generally where such entries are self-serving for the adversary or where they contain corrections or additions which are apparent even to the untrained eye. The most frequent questions raised with respect to such entries are: (1) Was something added or changed? (2) When, or in what order, was it written? (3) Was it written at the same time as the balance of the entry or record? and (4) Was it written by the same person who wrote some other entry or other portion of the record? Very rarely does the attorney question the authenticity of the complete record or major portions thereof. In some instances, the attorney's doubts as to the authenticity or accuracy of the medical records may be based not upon glaring corrections or additions, but rather upon inconsistencies between what his medical experts have advised him must have actually occurred and what the medical records indicate did occur. When counsel who handle medical malpractice cases encounter any of the aforementioned situations, the likelihood that physicians or hospital staff may have tampered with the records must be fully explored at the earliest opportunity.

To properly protect his client's interests and the integrity and credibility of his case, counsel should immediately submit the *entire* medical records to a reputable forensic document examiner. The document examiner should examine the complete record in a given case and not merely those entries that are of particular interest to the retaining attorney. In many instances, the attorney's suspicions may have been focused on detectable changes or additions that are either innocuous or that can be explained away legitimately on the basis of the record-keeper's customary manner of recordation. Oftentimes, the attorney has overlooked other portions of the record which may not have seemed material until the document examiner has inspected them and discovered some "hidden" irregularity which sheds new light on the case. For example, the expert may determine that pages of the record were substituted, thus raising the inference that pages containing damaging evidence are missing or were removed by doctors or nurses in an attempt to frustrate discovery of negligence or to avoid disciplinary action by superiors. This same careful scrutiny of documentary evidence must be employed by defense counsel as well because in the first place, it is essential to do so from a defensive standpoint, and secondly, because the perpetration of fraud and deceit with respect to documentary evidence in medical malpractice cases is not the exclusive province of defendants. There have been numerous cases where plaintiffs have altered or otherwise fraudulently prepared documentary evidence in an attempt to buttress an otherwise unmeritorious claim.

Whenever medical records or plaintiff-submitted documentary evidence is suspect, the wisdom of retaining a document expert prior to the deposition stage of the case cannot be overemphasized. By discovering the fraud well in advance of trial, the attorney can, through careful inquiry upon deposition, place his adversary in a most vulnerable position by pinning him or her to a recitation of facts which can be exposed as perjurious at trial. When this is accomplished, a successful verdict or a favorable settlement is virtually ensured because experience has taught lawyers that juries resent, and will penalize, attempted deception or concealment of the truth.

II. CASE HISTORY: FRAUDULENT ALTERATIONS IN HOSPITAL DISCHARGE SHEET

The mother of a brain-damaged boy who contracted bacterial meningitis in the hospital where he was born sued the hospital and the treating physician for medical malpractice. The child was born on September 4, 1974, and shortly thereafter the mother began complaining that the child was lethargic, had jaundice, and would not eat. The pediatrician said the mother was being hysterical and that it was just a formula problem. The mother and the child were discharged from the hospital on September 11, 1974, and the mother continued to call the doctor, complaining that the child was ill. The doctor never visited the child at home and insisted there was nothing wrong with the child.

On the advice of the child's grandmother, the child was taken to another hospital, where the child's condition was immediately diagnosed. The disease left the child with cerebral palsy, paralysis in an arm, and profound retardation. At age seven, the child was still unable to feed himself and was not toilet trained.

During the trial, the hospital and the treating physician contended that the child did not have obvious symptoms of infection and that although the child had tremors on the night prior to discharge from the hospital, the tremors had resolved by the time of discharge.

The hospital relied on the hospital records, as well as the testimony of the treating physician and hospital staff, to the effect that the child's symptoms, including the tremors, had resolved prior to the child's discharge from the hospital. The child's parents testified, however, that the child was not feeding well, was lethargic, and still had tremors even during and after discharge from the hospital.

Based upon the contradictions in the testimony at trial and apparent corrections and overwritings observed in the medical records, the plaintiff's attorney submitted the entire records to me for detailed examination.

Numerous corrections and additions to the record were detected, two of which proved crucial to the plaintiff's case. Both were contained in the Discharge Sheet filled out and signed by the treating physician.

The first such entry originally read, "Child has tremors since last night." This entry was altered by changing the "s" in "has" to a "d" and by obliterating (blacking out) the word "since" so that the corrected entry read, "Child had tremors last night." At the trial, the doctor claimed that this correction was made at the same time as the original entry. However, my findings and testimony demonstrated that two different pens were used, thus leading to the inference that the corrections were done at a different time than the original entry.

Handwriting examination and analysis also established that a second entry in the Discharge Sheet relating to a calcium test was made subsequent to the initial entries on the sheet. This proved to be significant because one justification used by the defendants for the discharge was that the child had a high calcium level, which would have been an alternative explanation for the tremors, thus indicating that the tremors were not necessarily indicative of an infection. Since it was established that the calcium level was not known by the doctor when she discharged the child, such justification could have been safely discounted by the jury and it was evident that this later entry could only have been made in an attempt to buttress the defendants' theory of the case.

After a three week trial, the jury returned a vedict for the plaintiff for an amount in excess of $5 million. *Scariati v. Flushing Hospital and Medical Center and Ruby Malva, M.D.*, Supreme Court, Queens County (1981).

III. CASE HISTORY: OFFICE RECORDS OF PLAINTIFF'S TREATING PHYSICIAN REVEAL FRAUDULENT ALTERATION

Plaintiff underwent surgery for repair of a hernia and subsequently sued the surgeon and the hospital for medical malpractice, alleging that as a result of their negligence, he had suffered a femoral nerve neuropathy on the right side which resulted in a permanent limp. The defendants acknowledged that the plaintiff had suffered a femoral nerve neuropathy and a limp but alleged that the neuropathy and the limp were temporary and that the patient's limp ceased four months after the operation.

During the presentation of plaintiff's direct case, his treating physician was called as a witness and testified that he had examined his office records covering a period of four years during which he had treated the plaintiff. Based upon a review of his records and his own physical examination of the plaintiff, it was his opinion that the plaintiff's limp was of a permanent nature.

Defense counsel requested a detailed forensic examination of the treating physician's office records in order to ascertain whether the sequential entries contained therein were written at one and the same time or over the four-year period during which the physician had treated the plaintiff. Based upon the examination of the records, there was no evidence to indicate that the entries were of recent vintage. In fact, most of the entries appeared to have been made at different times, thus eliminating the possibility that the records were reconstructed or rewritten at one time for litigation purposes. However, one of the pages of the physician's office records contained an entry under the heading of "Physical Examination" and careful inspection of said entry revealed that it had been altered. The original entry, which read "knee jerk *present*," had been changed to read "knee jerk *absent*." The treating physician attempted to explain this change as an inadvertent correction whereas defense counsel argued that the change was a fraudulent alteration made in an attempt to buttress plaintiff's claim that his limp was permanent instead of temporary.

The trial resulted in a hung jury and the case was subsequently settled for a nominal amount.

IV. CASE HISTORY: HOSPITAL RECORDS FRAUDULENTLY ALTERED

In a medical malpractice case brought against the City of New York, the plaintiff alleged that he was admitted to Queens General Hospital with a medical condition known as paranasal sinus infection. A complication ensued in the form of a cavernous sinus thrombosis, which can result in blindness and even death. The plaintiff alleged that the doctors in the hospital failed to diagnose his condition until seven days following his admission and that even after they made the proper diagnosis, they failed to give him penicillin in massive doses. Three days after the diagnosis was confirmed, the plaintiff became blind in one eye and three days later, he became blind in the other.

At the trial, the defense contended that when the patient entered the hospital, he had such an advanced case of cavernous sinus thrombosis that despite the loss of his sight, he was fortunate that his life could be saved. The hospital, relying on their own records for support, also alleged that once the patient's condition was diagnosed, he was given massive amounts of penicillin.

The hospital records were submitted by the plaintiff's attorney for forensic examination and the examination revealed that certain entries on the first page of the hospital record (i.e., patient put in an oxygen tent and given last rites of the church by a priest) were added at a later time to indicate that the patient's condition was critical when he was admitted to the hospital. Alterations in the record were also found with respect to the dosages of penicillin allegedly administered to the patient. They consisted of the following: (1) 1,000,000 units was altered to read 12,000,000 units by overwriting a figure "2" on the first zero, adding a zero at the end, and erasing the original commas and inserting two subsequent commas to indicate the greater amount; (2) 1,200,000 units was altered to read 12,000,000 units; (3) 2,000,000 units was altered to read 40,000,000 units; and (4) 2,000,000 units was altered to read 12,000,000 units.

The document examiner's testimony at the trial was accompanied by photographic exhibits which clearly demonstrated the alterations in the hospital records. The jury awarded the plaintiff $275,000 even though his weekly wages at the time of his illness amounted to only $106. No appeal was taken in the case. *Flanagan v. City of New York*, (Sup. Ct., 1969) (testimony from trial transcript).

V. CASE HISTORY: PLAINTIFF FRAUDULENTLY ALTERED LETTER RECEIVED FROM DEFENDANT-DOCTOR; OFFICE RECORDS OF PLAINTIFF'S FAMILY PHYSICIAN PROVED TO HAVE BEEN RECONSTRUCTED

Plaintiff sued a urologist for failure to make a timely diagnosis of a particular condition. A critical part of plaintiff's proof consisted of a typewritten form letter which was purportedly sent to the patient from the urologist's office in 1978 and which indicated that the results of the patient's urine tests were negative. The date, patient's name, and urologist's signature on the letter were handwritten in ballpoint pen.

Inasmuch as the defendant did not recall ordering any urine test for the patient in 1978, had no indications of such a test in his records, and did not remember signing the form letter in issue, defense counsel submitted the original form letter and certain comparison material, requesting me to determine whether the date, patient's name, and defendant's signature were written by the defendant or by any member of his office staff.

My examination and comparison of the relevant documents established that the form letter had, in fact, been dated, addressed, and signed by the defendant. However, the date on the letter had been altered by changing the figure "6" to an "8" so as to make the date of the letter appear to be 1978 instead of 1976, thus lending credence to the plaintiff's otherwise unmeritorious claim. The form letter was also found to be inconsistent with the typestyle and stationery used by the defendant in 1978.

The plaintiff in this case had also relied on the testimony and findings of her family physician, who had treated the plaintiff during the period from 1968 to 1979. This physician's office records were called into question as a result of certain entries describing symptoms which were inconsistent with the findings of the defendant-urologist.

Examination of these office records revealed that several pages of the records were reconstructed and substituted. In addition to an absence of normal variations in handwriting and undue uniformity in the pattern of the entries in question, which entries covered twelve office visits during a period of several months, there was a particular correction noted which could only be attributed to a rewriting process. The office visit for June 25th was dated by hand in the left-hand margin of the page. The subsequent office visit entered on that same page was for July 11th and was similarly dated by hand in the left-hand margin. Examination of the "June 25th" notation revealed an erasure of text underneath, which text was clearly deciphered to have originally read "July 11th," the very same date as the next office visit entered on that page. It was evident that a person would not mistake a date of July 11th for June 25th and that the error involved here could only have resulted from the physician's having recopied (and presumably reconstructed) a previously written record. These findings exposed the falsity of the family physician's claim that the records which he had presented were the original records and that he had recorded each of the entries in his records on the very same day that the patient had visited his office.

Disclosure of these discoveries before the court and opposing counsel resulted in a prompt dismissal of the plaintiff's lawsuit.

VI. CASE HISTORY: HOSPITAL RECORDS REVEAL ALTERED SPONGE COUNT AND FORGED SIGNATURE OF NURSE

A middle-aged housewife underwent an operation for a partial resection of the colon. During the post-operative phase, the woman suffered from severe abdominal pains which could not be accounted for medically. A second operation was performed, at which time a surgical sponge was discovered in her abdomen, apparently left there during the first operation on her colon. The sponge was removed during the second operation, and thereafter the woman sued the doctor and the hospital that performed the first operation for negligence.

The doctors and nurses testified that the standard instrument, needle and sponge count was performed during the operation and that it was routine procedure to make a count at two different times so as to ensure recovery of all instruments, needles and sponges. The operating room worksheet containing the sponge count was alleged to have been filled out by a single nurse during the operation, whose name and signature appeared on the worksheet.

Examination of the operating room worksheet revealed that two different ballpoint pens were used to enter the figures relating to the number of in-going and outgoing sponges and that the number relating to the outgoing sponge count had been altered (raised from "10" to "11") to make it correspond with the number of sponges that should have been removed from the plaintiff's abdomen. In addition to the alteration of the outgoing sponge count, it was discovered that the worksheet was not signed by the nurse whose name and purported signature appeared thereon and who was alleged to have maintained the sponge count throughout the operation. Rather, that nurse's name was signed by another nurse who had come into the operating room in the middle of the operation to replace the nurse who had started the sponge count. When the operation was completed, the second nurse evidently signed the first nurse's name to the worksheet covering the sponge count.

As a result of these findings by the document examiner, a favorable settlement was obtained by the plaintiff's attorney shortly before the trial was scheduled to commence.

VII. CASE HISTORY: FRAUDULENT ALTERATION IN MEDICATION SHEET; SUBSTITUTED PAGE IN DOCTOR'S ORDER SHEETS

The estate of a former patient instituted a wrongful death action against the hospital and the doctor involved in the treatment of the decedent prior to his death. The decedent had developed tetanus, which eventually proved fatal. The critical question in this case was whether the decedent was given tetanus antitoxin or tetanus toxoid. The plaintiff claimed that the decedent was given tetanus toxoid whereas the defendants maintained that tetanus antitoxin was administered. Both sides acknowledged that the standard of care in this particular case required that the patient be given tetanus antitoxin.

Examination of the hospital records revealed that there was an erasure in an entry on one of the medication sheets underneath the words "Tetanus Antitoxin." Microscopic examination and special photographic techniques revealed that "Tetanus Toxoid Fluid" were the original words entered into this record and that they were altered to read "Tetanus Antitoxin" by means of erasure and overwriting. The medical and legal significance of this change became readily apparent and it was now imperative to check the entire record for any entries which indicated that tetanus antitoxin was administered because any such entry would be inherently suspect in light of its self-serving purpose and the previously discovered alteration.

Upon examining the Doctor's Order Sheets, there was one page which contained six entries, each covering a different day, and each indicating that "patient (was) given tetanus antitoxin." Examination of these six entries showed no signs of alteration but instead revealed that all six entries were written "in one and the same sitting" and not at different times, as alleged by the defendants.

Further examination of the page containing these six entries proved even more enlightening. In comparing the hospital stencil imprint at the top of this page with the stencil imprint appearing at the top of every other page of the record, it was found to contain characteristics which were unique. Evidence at the trial established that a stencil bearing patient information is routinely affixed to numerous blank hospital record sheets numbered consecutively when the patient is admitted to the hospital. With the exception of the page containing the six self-serving entries, the stencil on each and every page of the hospital record was uniform in all respects. Thus, there could be no doubt that this page was substituted at some later time. The differences in the stencils were readily demonstrable to the jury. The routine stencil had abbreviated the patient's religion as "CATH." whereas the stencil on the substituted page abbreviated it as "CAT." Additionally, the alignment and punctuation of certain abbreviated words as they appeared in the routine stencil differed from the way they appeared in the stencil on the substituted page.

The document examiner's testimony and illustration to the jury of the alteration in the medication sheet and the substituted page in the doctor's order sheets proved to be so damaging to the defendants that the case was settled shortly thereafter for a substantial sum of money.

VIII. CONCLUSION

It is hoped that the foregoing case histories have provided the reader with some of the more prevalent types of alterations, additions, and substitutions of medical records that can be discovered by the forensic document examiner and illustrated by demonstrative evidence. As stated at the outset, this article is by no means intended to be exhaustive of this subject matter. The reader should be advised that in the course of detecting fraud with respect to documentary evidence, the forensic document examiner employs various other examination techniques involving the analysis of handwriting; typewriting; paper; ink lines; folds, holes and tears in paper; impressions or lack of impressions on paper; ink offsets or lack of offsets on the reverse side of a given page; intersecting ink lines or the reaction of ink lines intersecting folds, holes or tears in paper; and sometimes even photocopies and their identifying characteristics. Techniques for establishing the relative date of a given document can also be employed to establish a discrepancy between the purported date of preparation and the actual date of preparation of the document.

By being alert to possible alterations, additions and substitutions of entries in medical records, the attorney handling a medical malpractice case can pinpoint those instances where detailed examination of the records by a forensic document examiner would be beneficial. In the case of his own client's records, the attorney will be better prepared to evaluate his own position in the lawsuit. In the case of his adversary's records, the attorney will be better prepared to refute his adversary's allegations and documentary evidence.

Grateful appreciation is extended to Matthew Bender and Hanna Sulner for portions of this article.

CHAPTER THREE

DRUGS IN MEDICAL MALPRACTICE LITIGATION

Henry R. Simon, R. Ph., J.D.

I. DETERMINATION OF POTENTIAL DEFENDANTS: THEORIES OF LIABILITY

A. Physician

The Federal Food Drug & Cosmetic Act and New York State law mandate that certain drugs may be dispensed only upon prescription of a duly licensed physician. The physician serves as the "learned intermediary" in the chain of distribution for those products which are deemed to be of sufficient potency, toxicity, or potential danger as to require careful evaluation by the physician of the patient's condition and proper indication for use of a specific drug. The decision to prescribe a particular drug must be based upon a reasonably careful history, physical examination, and documentation of signs and symptoms which would support the use of a specific pharmaceutical agent. Of equal importance, the physician should become aware of any pre-existing condition which would contraindicate the use of a drug. For example, a physician who selected an antibiotic for treatment of an infection which was caused by bacteria resistant to that antibiotic would clearly be guilty of malpractice once the results of the culture and sensitivity (C and S) series have been made available, provided of course the physician did not switch the patient to the appropriate antibiotic promptly after receiving the C and S results.

Although a physician need not possess an encyclopedic memory of all facts pertaining to all commonly used drugs, he should indeed be familiar with those drugs which are prescribed for the patient and the potential side effects and hazards associated with their use, including dangers of interaction with other drugs or even food products.

The mere presence of an unfavorable side effect or drug reaction does not—itself—provide a basis for imposing liability automatically on the prescribing physician. However, the following are some frequent bases for physician liability associated with prescription drugs:

1. Failure to keep up with medical literature regarding side effects (Example: prescription of potent and potentially dangerous antibiotics for trivial infections);

2. Failure to take comprehensive history of other drugs causing drug interactions (Example: prescription of Coumadin blood thinners to a patient

who is taking aspirin-containing products which potentiate anticoagulant properties inducing hemorrhage);

3. Failure to monitor patient for early signs of drug-related injury and promptly discontinue medication (Example: administration of ototoxic antibiotics of the aminoglycoside group without monitoring kidney function may induce deafness if renal output is substantially impaired);

4. Failure to obtain informed consent (Example: use of an established pharmaceutical product for therapeutic indications not approved by the Food & Drug Administration);

5. Failure to give adequate instructions to patient regarding drug use (Example: prescription of potent antihistamines which induce drowsiness without giving specific instructions not to drive, operate machinery, etc.).

B. Pharmaceutical Manufacturer

The drug manufacturer has a duty to adequately test its product for safety prior to marketing. The Federal Food Drug & Cosmetic Act requires that the manufacturer test for safety and efficacy. 21 U.S.C. sec. 355(b)(1)(1970).

The duty to test is dependent upon the foreseeable risk of harm to potential users in light of current scientific and medical knowledge.

The pharmaceutical company is under a duty to warn *the physician*, rather than the patient, of risks and dangers that might be associated with use of a drug. The rationale for this is that the physician is the "learned intermediary" in the chain of distribution and must make professional decisions on whether a patient's condition requires a particular drug, the proper dosage, etc.

The pharmaceutical company has a duty to warn the prescribing physician of all risks and dangers that it is aware of or, in the exercise of reasonable care, should be aware of with respect to side effects and toxicity of the drug.

The drug company has also been held to be under a duty to warn a treating physician as well as the prescribing physician, where it can reasonably be anticipated that a treating physician might be more likely to observe the actual symptoms of a drug's untoward consequences. *McEwen v. Ortho Pharmaceutical Corp.*, 270 Or. 375, 528 P.2d 522 (1974).

Stated another way, a manufacturer has a duty to warn of adverse reactions which the manufacturer knows, or has reason to know, are inherent to the use of its drug. *Woodhill v. Parke Davis & Company*, 58 Ill. App. 3d 349, 374 N.E.2d 683 (1978).

The manufacturer's duty to warn is commensurate with actual knowledge gained from research, adverse reaction reports, and the manufacturer's constructive knowledge as measured by scientific literature and other medical communications. The pharmaceutical manufacturer is treated as an expert in its particular field and is under a continuing duty to keep abreast of scientific developments which effect the product.

A drug warning must be included in the "product labeling" of the drug, which includes all advertisements, *Physician Desk Reference* entries, and journal ads. The detail (sales) force may, on occasion, nullify an otherwise adequate warning in the product literature by overpromotion to the physician. *Stevens v. Parke Davis & Company*, 9 Cal. 3d 51, 107 Cal. Rptr. 45, 507 P.2d 653 (1973).

The warning of side effects must be timely communicated to the prescribing and treating physician as soon as the manufacturer reasonably learns of a risk.

A pharmaceutical manufacturer may be held liable for an innocent misrepresentation if the misrepresentation is material and was relied upon by the prescribing physician, Restatement 2d of Torts Sec. 402B. Thus, where a drug manufacturer represented its drug to be free and safe from all dangers of addiction and a treating physician relied upon that representation, the manufacturer was strictly liable when the representation proved to be false and harm resulted. *Crocker v. Winthrop Laboratories*, 514 S.W. 2d 429 (Texas 1974).

A difficult question is whether to bring an action against the prescribing physician and the pharmaceutical company. If the side effect is well established in the literature, e.g., anaphylactic reaction to penicillin, the manufacturer will almost never be held liable if that reaction occurs because the physician knew or, in the exercise of reasonable care, should have known, that certain individuals are allergic to penicillin and it should not be prescribed for those persons. On the other hand, if a new semisynthetic penicillin derivative is introduced on the market and does not contain adequate warnings that there might be cross-sensitivity to penicillin in allergic individuals, the prescribing physician may not have had adequate information when he prescribed the product, hence there might be a cause of action against the manufacturer for failure to provide an adequate warning of the cross-sensitivity.

C. Pharmacist

1. General Duty of Dispensing Pharmacist

A druggist must use "reasonable care" in filling prescriptions. Because of the potentially grave danger of dispensing errors, the duty has been described as "the highest degree of care in filling prescriptions." *Troppi v. Scarf*, 31 Mich. App. 240, 187 N.W.2d 511 (1971); *Burke v. Bean*, 363 S.W. 2d 366 (Tex. Civ. App. 1962).

A retail pharmacist has generally not been held liable for breach of implied warranties of fitness and merchantability for dispensing prescribed drugs. In *Bichler v. Willing*, 58 A.D.2d 331, 397 N.Y.S.2d 57 (1st Dep't 1977), the pharmacist was not liable on a strict products liability theory.

Likewise, pharmacists generally have not been held liable for failure to warn the consumer of potential side effects from prescription drugs since that role has been generally reserved for the physician serving as a learned intermediary whose responsibility includes the selection of a proper therapeutic agent and discussion with the patient pertaining to information necessary for safe use of that product.

There are, however, certain instances where the pharmacist might be liable. The most common areas are discussed below.

2. Pharmacist's Liability for Dispensing Improper Drugs

This error occurs most frequently when the pharmacist misreads the physician's prescription, which is often scribbled and barely legible. Where the pharmacist is not certain of exactly what the prescribing physician has ordered, the pharmacist is under a duty to call and obtain clarification from the physician. The failure to verify the precise drug prescribed is a departure from accepted standards of good pharmacy practice.

3. Errors in Dosage

A pharmacist will be liable for dispensing the wrong dosage of medication where the pharmacist has misread an unclear prescription and failed to verify the proper dosage. This may be especially important with the prescription of drugs administered in minute dosages, such as cardiac drugs, including Digoxin and Digitoxin, which are prescribed in tablets containing only a fraction of a milligram per tablet. Misplacing the decimal point even one place can have fatal results.

Most drugs have standard dosages set by the manufacturer and the Federal Food & Drug Administration. However, the prescribing physician must make the final decision on dosages and there are legitmate therapeutic indications where greater than the recommended dosage might be required in a particular situation. Nonetheless, if the dispensing pharmacist receives a prescription for a dosage which appears to be in the toxic range, it can reasonably be argued that the pharmacist is under a duty to call and verify an unusually high dosage or what appears to be an error in the frequency of administration. The pharmacist's technical training and knowledge of pharmacology impose a high duty to be aware of toxic levels of drugs and, to the extent they might prove to be injurious, at least call the physician and verify that a particular dosage is in fact what the physician wants in that case. A common example of a potential for serious harm occurs with a prescription by a pediatrician for an infant where the dosage was substantially in excess of that usually recommended in pediatric care.

4. Liability for Excessive Prescription Refills

Generally, the physician will indicate on the prescription the number of refills allowed without the necessity of the pharmacist contacting the physician for permission to refill. The number of refills may be limited by federal statute for controlled drugs such as narcotics and barbiturates, as well as other potential drugs of abuse such as certain tranquilizers.

The pharmacist should strictly follow the orders of the prescribing physician with respect to number of refills permitted and, if the patient requests a refill where none is indicated on the prescription form, the pharmacist is under a duty to contact the physician and obtain permission prior to granting a refill.

An area of potential liability occurs with drugs which may induce injury from long-term usage. Notwithstanding that the physician may have authorized the patient to refill the drug indefinitely (noted as "PRN" on the prescription), the pharmacist should be alert that there are indeed certain drugs which by their very nature may cause serious harm if used continuously. For example, certain drugs used to treat migraine headaches may cause cardiac fibrosis (build-up of scar tissue on the heart), if administered continuously. If the pharmacist sees that the prescription is being refilled every month for many months, or even years, it can be argued that the pharmacist should consult the physician and determine if the physician in fact wants this practice to continue. This is especially true where the pharmacist has received package inserts in the medication advising that the drug should not be used continously without "drug holidays." In this sense, the pharmacist serves as a double check on the physician based upon the pharmacist's extensive knowledge and training in the field of drug actions.

D. Hospital

There is an extensive chain of distribution of drugs in the hospital setting and departures by workers in several professional disciplines have formed the basis of liability for drug-induced injury in the hospital.

The hospital based pharmacist is responsible for ordering and storing drugs, as well as dispensing them based upon prescription of the physician. In the hospital setting, however, there is usually an additional check on the physician's order since the prescription is usually administered by the nurse based upon an order placed in the chart. If the pharmacist dispenses the wrong product or an incorrect dosage, liability will arise and the hospital will be responsible. However, in some hospital settings because of staffing problems it is not uncommon for persons other than registered nurses to administer drugs on the wards. These persons might include nurses' aides and orderlies, whose formal training, if any, may have little bearing on proper drugs and dosages.

II. RECOGNITION OF DRUG-INDUCED INJURY

A. Diagnosis of Drug-Related Disease

Adverse drug reactions are among the most difficult diagnoses for a physician to make. Most patients who experience drug reactions are receiving multiple drugs and are also suffering from one or more underlying illnesses that might account for their symptoms. In addition, many of the symptoms of drug side effects (e.g., headaches, nausea, dizziness, and fever) are subjective and nonspecific.

Long-term effects of drugs may not be seen until years after they have been administered, making causation difficult to prove. Moreover, maximal concentration of drugs that accumulate in certain tissues (e.g., antimalarial drugs in the lens of the eyes) may not be reached until drug administration has actually terminated and may remain elevated for prolonged periods of time so the damage may be caused after the offending drug has been discontinued.

Sometimes, an adverse drug reaction will not be noted as such in the patient's medical record. Faced with a suspicious death or an unexplained serious reaction, it may be necessary to look back at the event from different medical prospectives (e.g., gynecologic, neurologic, or hematologic) to identify laboratory data or new symptoms that do not "fit" into the anticipated course of the disease and which may be indicative of a failure to monitor or a failure to integrate adequately the patient's clinical symptoms in the diagnostic work-up. The picture may be even further complicatd by the not uncommon practice of unwittingly prescribing drugs to treat symptoms of a developing drug reaction. This will compound the problem where the second drug administered also has side effects further confusing the clinical picture.

B. Liability for Different Types of Drug Reactions

Drugs can cause injury by one of several mechanisms. Depending upon the specific reaction, the liable party might be the prescribing physician, the pharmaceutical manufacturer, the pharmacist, or in some instances, support a finding of contributory negligence by the plaintiff.

The following are six common types of drug-related injuries which will be discussed individually:

1. Toxic
2. Hypersensitivity
3. True Allergic
4. Idiosyncratic
5. Teratogenic
6. Carcinogen

1. The toxic injury is frequently related to the dosage administered or a cumulative effect from prolonged administration of the drug. From the standpoint of liability, the key factor is *predictability.* Thus, an excessive dose of the heart drug Digoxin is toxic and has been recognized as such for many years in the medical literature. The liable party would be the prescribing physician or, if the pharmacist made a dosage administration error in filling the prescription, the pharmacist. Another example would be the administration of Indocin or Butazolidin which, when administered over prolonged periods of time, are known to cause blood dyscrasias which may be fatal. The physician must carefully monitor the patient and require periodic blood counts when administering these drugs. Failure to do so has been the basis for liability in several malpractice cases. As to the pharmaceutical manufacturer, the side effects of these drugs are clearly recognized and established and generally are the subject of comprehensive warnings in the product literature, including the package insert, reducing the potential for liability.

2. The hypersensitive reaction refers to an abnormally increased sensitivity an individual may have to administration of a certain drug. This will cause a patient to experience increased or exaggerated effects of that drug as compared with administration of a similar dosage to other persons. An example of this would be certain individuals experiencing profound drowsiness with the administration of small dosages of antihistamines where a similar dose administered to most patients would not cause any significant sleepiness. Another type of reaction is orthostatic hypotension caused by the administration of certain antihypertensive drugs such as Methyldopa. This reaction causes precipitous drop in blood pressure often creating a sensation of light headedness and occasionally even fainting. The physician who prescribes these drugs for a patient for the first time should be alert to these possibilities and advise the patient to exercise caution and avoid driving or operating machinery until the individual has determined his reaction to these medications. Again, this type of side effect is generally recognized in a limited percentage of patients and is usually the subject of some warning in the pharmaceutical literature accompanying the drug. The liability for injury would generally lie with the physician.

3. The term "allergic" has been used loosely to refer to all types of drug reactions. In fact, a true allergic reaction is a response elicited by a drug sometime after an allergic state has been established. Anaphylactoid reaction to penicillin or sulfa drugs will occur only after the individual has been

previously exposed to the same or a similar drug and the body has been "sensitized." Thereafter, the administration of even minute quantities of the drug may induce a full-blown allergic reaction of the devastating anaphylactoid type including constriction of the trachea, hives, wheezing, and swelling. It may lead to inability to breath or profound shock, sometimes leading to death. Drugs which cause allergic reactions have, for the most part, been identified and most package inserts have product literature from the pharmaceutical company which makes reference to this characteristic of the drug. The physician must take an adequate and detailed drug history to elicit a prior allergic reaction to drugs. This requires more than a brief off-the-cuff inquiry as to whether the person is allergic to any drugs and might require a more detailed series of questions delving into whether the person has had any reaction from drugs or foods or is an allergic individual with history of hay fever, food allergies, or similar conditions. The physician should be especially alert to a patient who complains of itching, hives, watering of the eyes, or wheezing following the administration of any drug. In cases where the drug has a substantial potential for drug allergy, the patient should specifically be advised to immediately discontinue the drug upon the appearance of the any of these symptoms and contact the physician immediately. This is almost mandatory where the patient has never been administered that class of drugs, such as certain of the penicillin derivatives, on any previous occasion.

4. The term "idiosyncratic" reaction has been loosely used to refer to many types of rare drug reactions. In fact, the term "idiosyncratic" technically refers to an uncharacteristic response in an individual to a drug caused by some constitutional aberration in the recipient, such as a metabolic defect or enzyme deficiency which causes that individual to have a serious adverse reaction to the drug. This is distinguished from a hypersensitive reaction because with hypersensitivity the pharmacologic reaction is exaggerated, but expected. With idiosyncrasy there is a totally different response to a drug. For example, certain individuals, because of constitutional makeup, lack some enzymes which break down the drug. Without these enzymes, the drug can remain unchecked in the body causing serious injury. For example, the sulfonylurea class of drugs which includes the oral antidiabetic drugs may cause the body to break down red blood cells unless the person has sufficient levels of an enzyme known as 6-Glucose PD. It may even result in an acute hemolytic crisis. This seems to occur much more commonly in blacks and it has been suggested that prior to administering these drugs the physician should conduct a relatively simple test to determine if the individual has that enzyme deficiency. The liability would lie with the physician if he does not advise

the patient to report certain early signs of this reaction such as petechial hemorrhage characterized by red blotches on the skin. There may also be a basis for liability against the pharmaceutical manufacturer if it has not been given an adequate warning of this reaction in its product literature. In sum, the term "idiosyncratic" has been used as a catch-all phrase and is currently confused with idiopathic reaction which refers to a mechanism of unknown origin. From the standpoint of products liability, the term idiosyncratic has been used in an attempt to show the product itself was not defective but there was some defect in the recipient which, in rare cases, would cause injury. In contemporary products liability litigation, the central question is whether the product contained an adequate warning of the potential harm. A factor in this analysis is how frequently it causes this type of reaction and the determination of whether the warning is adequate is usually left for the jury.

5. The teratogenic injury is defined as the production of drug-induced physical defects in the fetus during fetal development. The defects may be immediately apparent after birth (such as with thalidomide) or after developmental delay when the conditions might manifest themselves years later in adolescence or adulthood. An example of this would be those reproductive abnormalities allegedly associated with prenatal adminstration of DES (Diethylstilbestrol). Liability may fall on either the prescribing physician or the drug company. If a drug has recognized teratologic potential, the drug would obviously be contraindicated in pregnancy or even in women of childbearing age since they might be pregnant. On the other hand, if the physician is treating a serious condition such as cancer, the use of teratogenic antimetabolite anticancer drugs might still be indicated where there is no other treatment available and after there has been full discussion of the possible risks with the patient. The Federal Food & Drug Administration has recently characterized the potential risk to offspring for many drugs. In most instances, the potential effect is unknown resulting in the general admonition to the effect that the drug has not been proved safe for use in pregnancy and should only be used when potential benefits outweigh the risks.

If the product was prescribed many years before the teratologic effects became recognized, liability would not accrue to the physician but to the pharmaceutical company if there was a failure to warn of known side effects or a failure to test for those which might reasonably be anticipated.

6. A carcinogen is any agent or substance which produces cancer or accelerates the development of cancer. The estrogens have frequently been cited

as potentially carcinogenic increasing the incidence and rate of tumor formation in the uterus. Generally, the physician who prescribes substances such as estrogens with the potential (albeit disputed) for increased cancer formation, such as cancer of the uterus, should discuss this potential with the patient and allow the patient to arrive at an informed decision whether or not to use the product. The benefit versus risk analysis is important in this context. However, if a physician detects what might be benign or malignant mammary nodules, and prescribes estrogens without determining whether in fact a mammary cancer is present, the physician will be liable if the patient has an estrogen dependent neoplasia, the growth of which will be rapidly accelerated with estrogen administration. The pharmaceutical company might also be liable if the product did not contain an adequate warning of the cancer potential.

C. Injuries Caused by Drug Interactions

This occurs when one drug modifies the action of another causing the patient to respond more or less intensely to one of the drugs than normal or in a manner different from that expected.

A common and dangerous interaction is the administration of antihistamines with the consumption of alcohol. Antihistamines, by their nature, tend to induce drowsiness in many individuals. This effect is dramatically increased with even slight consumption of alcohol creating a dangerous situation for individuals driving an automobile or operating machinery. Likewise, the administration of certain common tranquilizers may interact with antihistamines potentiating the effect of both and inducing substantial drowsiness. A pharmacist who dispenses a prescription for potent tranquilizers and prescription antihistamines should be aware of this interaction and advise the consumer to be alert for such a potential problem.

Another dangerous interaction occurs when a cardiac patient is prescribed anticoagulant drugs ("blood thinners") following certain types of myocardial infarctions. Many of these anticoagulants, such as Coumadin, will have their anticoagulating effects enhanced tremendously with the administration of even a single aspirin tablet. Accordingly, the pharmacist should be alert to dispensing prescriptions for Coumadin and concommitantly filling a prescription for any aspirin-containing prescription product. Based upon the pharmacist's extensive training in the field of pharmacology and drug interaction, one can reasonably argue that the pharmacist should be under a duty to be aware of common and serious drug interactions and advise the consumer to avoid using certain "over-the-counter" drug products or to consult with the physician prior to purchasing and using such products when taking specific prescription drugs. This is especially true where individuals may receive and present to the pharmacist prescriptions from multiple physicians. The pharmacist might be the only individual with knowledge of exactly what medications were being dispensed simultaneously to fill prescriptions from different practitioners.

The potential for such danger has motivated states to enact Patient Profile Systems which must be monitored by the retail pharmacist. The Patient Profile System (PPS) is mandated under New Jersey State Law and in other jurisdictions. In essence, they require the dispensing pharmacist to keep an accurate record of every drug that is dispensed to a patient on individual patient file cards. This will alert the pharmacist to potential drug interactions and instances where a person may be obtaining muliple drugs of abuse from numerous physicians. The PPS enables the pharmacist to anticipate potential drug interaction problems and call the prescribing physician where indicated to prevent possible injury to a consumer.

CHAPTER FOUR

THE PHYSICIAN AND THE MALPRACTICE SUIT

Richard J. Coburn, D.M.D., M.D., J.D.

I. INTRODUCTION

Without question, most physicians are distraught over the vagaries and complexities of a malpractice suit from beginning to end. Metropolitan doctors who are overexposed to legal challenges or who elect to testify frequently may be exceptions, but for the average physician, a malpractice suit is one of the most unsettling experiences in his professional career. From a legal viewpoint, the physician's dilemma and his response are out of proportion to the occasion. Nevertheless, the wound is deep and the physician's behavior throughout the suit is dictated by this pain. The legal community must be cognizant of this reaction. We lawyers realize the plaintiff attorney is simply "doing his thing," much as the surgeon "cuts," and the psychiatrist "shrinks." This analogy has no practical application. Like the frogs in Plutarch's *Water and Land Animals*, the physicians are often dying in earnest.

The conflict begins with the seeming incompatibility between medicine's countless unknowns and the law's well-defined but "grey" legal principles. Combine this with the physician's nearly impossible task of informing the patient of all medical possibilities and the impracticality of recording everything which transpires in the doctor/patient relationship, and one begins to appreciate the quicksand footing with which most physicians view lawsuits. For example, I have been sued on several occasions for scars following elective surgery. I am sure the plaintiff's lawyers felt in each case that a legitimate instance of malpractice existed, that is the patient undertook elective surgery to improve her appearance and was left instead with unsatisfactory scars. Yet any surgeon can relate that the differences in patient healing are vast and subject to no absolute standard. Scars range from the ideal fine white line to the cauliflower excretions of a keloid. It is hoped the surgeon closes the wounds in a workmanlike manner. Frankly, it is just as easy to close it well as not. Yet when a scar is less than perfect, the patient is justifiably distressed. The surgeon may attempt a revision and may or may not achieve the sought-after result. At this point, assuming the scar is unacceptable to the patient, a lawyer is consulted and a decision is made to sue. The surgeon feels he has done his best, his pride is hurt, his ego tarnished and, depending on the magnitude of the problem, resentment is all-consuming. It is within this fragile framework that the plaintiff's and defendant's attorneys encounter the physician. The defense lawyer must have the bedside manner of yesteryear to overcome hostility and find a means of invoking cooperation.

In this chapter the relationship between the doctor and defense lawyer will be considered in detail. In addition, the issues relating to preparing the physician for trial— records, timing, ancillary personnel, strategy and delays— will be examined.

II. THE INITIAL CONTACT

The original sin often relates to the medical malpractice insurance carrier. The physician reports the service of process and is promptly assigned a legal firm to begin the defense. The well-sued doctor may request a legal office with whom he or she is well acquainted, but this is not usually the scenario. In most legal conflicts, the family lawyer is consulted and the matter is handled expeditiously or the problem is referred to a chosen colleague with whom a similar alliance is quickly established. In this most crucial alleged malpractice, the two parties are, more often than not, complete strangers. The "system" unwittingly creates a built-in obstacle between the physician and his counsel. Ideally, the physician should consult with several legal firms specializing in defense and make a personal informed selection. Then, when a suit arises, there is an established relationship on which to build. Few physicians have pursued this unusual course and it is important for the lawyer to appreciate this gap in the selection process. This is especially true if the lawyer is a young, junior member of the firm, dealing with an older doctor. The lawyer should expect some initial lack of cooperation. The physician will often behave as though his head was in the proverbial sand, hoping the nightmare will go away if it cannot be seen or felt. The lawyer's telephone call, or worse, that of his secretary or legal aide, serves as a harsh reminder that this method only works for the ostrich.

The first contact between the lawyer and doctor arises when the physician is called to obtain the data necessary to construct a legal answer to the suit. If it is the doctor's first lawsuit, the lawyer may be quite surprised by the distress, hostility and fear. At least, be prepared to handle these emotions. The lawyer must remember that most physicians know little of pleadings and answers and will need a mini-course in the anatomy of a lawsuit. It is desirable to impart an overview of the events which will happen in the next few weeks, months, or even years, particularly in Manhattan or a similar metropolitan area. The importance of this first exchange between the lawyer and doctor cannot be overemphasized. It will set the tone for the entire relationship, for while it is perfunctory business for the lawyer, it is traumatic for the doctor.

The concept of an early meeting in the doctor's environment may be unusual but could yield rewards far in excess of the energy expended. Consider the merits of the lawyer visiting the physician's office, immediately placing the doctor at ease and conducting the interview in the milieu where he or she is accustomed to answering questions. These familiar surroundings will insure that the data gathering process will be vastly superior to the usual alternative—the doctor arriving at the lawyer's busy office, hat in hand. Secondly, the visit provides the lawyer with insight into the temperament of his client from the tone of the office, through and including the physician's appearance and demeanor. Thirdly, the lawyer will have a fresh look at the office, the clinic and the hospital records, plus the staff. The lawyer's assessment will be most helpful in evaluating the doctor's legal position. Finally, the visit provides the physician with the sense of a team working together on his behalf. It should be no surprise that the overall image of lawyers held by the medical profession is tarnished. In New York County, every single issue of the Medical Society Bulletin addresses the malpractice problem, the Society's attempt to gain reform, and the Legislature's failure to cooperate. Rightly or wrongly, physicians perceive the New York Legislature as being dominated by lawyers dedicated to protecting their own. Even defense lawyers are tainted with this brush. They may be on the "side of the angels," but they have to prove it.

A collateral benefit to this recommended office visit is the positive influence it can have on the lawyer's practice. One can be certain that should the physician or his associates have another medical/legal problem, this concerned lawyer will be retained. The under thirty-five year old lawyer who introduced me to this method is now busier than most of his more seasoned colleagues. This primary contact, be it by telephone, mail, or actual visit, completes the first phase of the doctor/lawyer relationship: the gathering of information to answer the pleadings. For the physician, the whole affair is likely to be tucked away in a remote memory bank only to occasionally resurface like a bad dream.

III. EXAMINATION BEFORE TRIAL

Barring interrogatories, the next step involving doctor participation focuses on the Examination Before Trial (E.B.T.). Traditionally, this is the doctor's first meeting with his defense attorney and not infrequently it is a hurried affair scheduled only hours before the hearing. If this chapter discourages this scenario, a tremendous hurdle in a medical/legal relationship will have been overcome. Nothing disturbs the physician more than to receive a call from the lawyer's secretary attempting to schedule the Examination and the preliminary conference within the week. The restraints of bringing two or more busy professionals together dictates that the pre-E.B.T. conference be scheduled well in advance of the actual confrontation. Similarly, scheduling at the mutual convenience of the attorney and the physician and with plenty of notice gives continuity to the previously established image of a well-orchestrated defense team. It dispels the all too common impression that the defense awoke only after the plaintiff decided to proceed.

It is advantageous to hold the pre-E.B.T. meeting in the lawyer's office and preferably in the environment where the actual examination will take place. Time spent in E.B.T. preparation will yield dividends throughout the trial. It is the first adversarial encounter and confidence is as important as sound facts and records. The lawyer should keep in mind how he or she would feel if the surgeon were about to remove a cancer. The surgeon has excised hundreds; the lawyer has never faced life-threatening surgery before. If it is the physician's first E.B.T. and the lawyer's hundredth, the lawyer must try to reverse the roles.

There is no magic formula for preparing the physician defendant for an E.B.T. If the lawyer took advantage of an early office consultation, he will most likely have an impression of the client's ability to handle the situation. Unquestionably, a major factor relates to the complexity of the suit—the treatment rendered and the severity of the end result. For example, in defending an obstetrician or anesthetist versus a brain-damaged child, the emotional involvement for all concerned is a major obstacle to be resolved regardless of the specifics. The physician will harbor ongoing feelings of guilt and remorse, not necessarily for the treatment, but surely for the outcome. Here, the doctor/lawyer relationship will be significantly more intense than in a suit over a resultant scar.

The most critical element in E.B.T. preparation is that the doctor is apprehensive of the unknown. If it is the tenth E.B.T. for a given physician, this tension may be less, depending on the circumstances of the case. The lawyer must never forget that he is the "protector." He must, to the best of his ability, communicate this "guardian-like" quality. If he can project this confidence, the rest will fall into place. The lawyer's role here is to prepare the physician in all facets of the E.B.T.—the practical considerations, the psychological, the strategy—and thereby dispel the unknown demons. Plaintiff lawyers frequently focus on informed consent. Reverse the role: review the E.B.T. like you would have wanted your client to have explained the operative or medical procedure.

A final thought on E.B.T. protocol: if the lawyer has any rapport with the plaintiff's counsel, an attempt should be made to schedule the date and hour when it will not be cancelled. Physicians have no knowledge and less feeling for the lawyer's chaotic schedule. A physician's emergencies are routine compared to the vagaries of legal appearances, but the doctor is unaware. Similarly, the physician's appointments must be rearranged around the E.B.T.; patients must be rescheduled, surgery cancelled and emergencies referred elsewhere. To follow this necessary office disruption with a last minute cancellation by your secretary destroys all previously generated good will. The lawyer must forewarn his client that cancellations occur, and then attempt through compromising, cajoling, and just good luck to fix a date on which all can attend. Even the plaintiff's attorney may be rewarded by finding a more cooperative defendant. The doctor's presumption that repeated delays are designed for his inconvenience would be negated.

IV. TRIAL PREPARATION

If the E.B.T. was thoroughly researched and orchestrated, this phase should be more a psychological exercise. The idea of an encounter session evokes a mental as well as a physical commitment, and that is exactly what it should be, without telephone interruptions and the like. Typically, encounter groups gather on weekends in semi-seclusion free from distractions. Likewise, trial preparation should take place in the lawyer's office at the end of the day, at lunch or, if appropriate, dinner. Obviously the intensity of preparation will vary with the magnitude of the case, the issues and the personalities involved, but the principles are valid. Remember, the courtroom is likely to be as foreign to the doctor as the operating room is to the lawyer. And the doctor must arrive unsedated! The physician is the variable and the lawyer must be equipped to identify and separate facts, ego and emotions before combining these forces into a defense strategy. There is no single calculus. It parallels the physician-patient relationship where there is always an emotional component to an illness. The concerned physician, by trial and error, and occasionally training, learns to treat both. The lawyer's task is similar and success will be proportional to one's experience and "desk-side" manner.

Physicians' records merit a separate consideration. Assuming they are legible, they are still woefully inadequate by legal standards. The reasons are numerous: bad habits, the nature of medicine, and mostly likely the plain and simple limitations of time. The physician with ten hospital patients visits each for five to ten minutes; the legal mind would not think a five-minute note on each one unreasonable. For most physicians, however, this extra hour does not exist. Similarly, when a new patient is seen in the office, the consultations lasts thirty to fourty-five minutes. From a legal viewpoint, it is unlikely that the most conscientious medical notes would be acceptable. This recordation problem makes the informed consent issue troublesome. The physician knows the patient must be informed regarding the contemplated treatment, the alternatives and the complications. Litigation lawyers and doctors are familiar with studies showing how little patients hear and how rapidly they forget. Thus, the legal documentation is of great importance but one that medicine in the 1980s has yet to solve. Videotaping of the interview has been discussed, but few have moved this far. The use of literature and informative videotapes on specific procedures, such as cardiac catheterizations, hernias, and cosmetic surgery, is increasing. Perhaps the doctor glut predicted for the 1990s will lower patient volume and permit the legal principles of contract to impact on physicians' offices.

The legal considerations of preparing the defense are discussed in far more detail in following chapters. The purpose here is to encourage lawyers to use the physician more fully. In a weak case, the doctor likely holds the key to winning. In a strong case against the doctor, he or she may or may not be able to help the defense. If the lawyer calls frantically a week before the trial concerning an incident which occurred five to seven years ago, it is unrealistic to expect much help. At this point, the lawyer has little alternative but to "wing it" and let the plaintiff win or lose on the strength or weakness of his or her expertise.

In the alternative, the lawyer has established good rapport early in the case, the team has worked closely together on the E.B.T. and has maintained contact. It follows that trial preparation will proceed smoothly. The lawyer will begin by reviewing every facet of the case and formalizing the issues. He should have organized his approach and committed it to writing. Despite their recordkeeping, most physicians are well-organized, slightly to severely compulsive men and women. This is especially true for surgeons who traditionally have the most suits. A systematic approach by the lawyer will insure a meeting of the minds. A conference arranged well in advance of the trial, in a tranquil interruption-free setting, possibly at the physician's convenience, will enhance the team's approach. Little else will be done at the doctor's convenience when the battle heats up, so at this juncture deferring to the physician will build good will. The doctor will need a mini-course on the art of trial advocacy. Despite being overeducated, most physicians have absolutely no knowledge of courtroom activity, protocol or schedules. They rarely sit on juries, often missing this opportunity for indoctrination. The lawyer must assume ignorance and instruct accordingly. To enlist the physician's complete support in the defense, the lawyers should review the pleadings and like a good informed consent, outline the strategy and options. It is hoped this will stimulate the physician's enthusiasm and he or she will become active in all phases of the defense.

Frequently the physician can be helpful in suggesting and providing reading material to further enlighten the lawyer's background and preparation. It would not be inappropriate for the lawyer to borrow meaningful texts or even to hold the doctor responsible for securing needed references. Each relationship will be different; some physicians will relish the campaign and eagerly support the lawyer's research efforts. Some will even initiate their own. Others will prefer the "ostrich" stance mentioned earlier. There is no question that the lawyer's interest and enthusiasm alone will convert a few nonbelievers.

We finally come to the day in court. Fortunately, despite apprehension, lack of exposure and occasionally hurried preparation, most physicians are good witnesses in their own defense. The reason is not profound—physicians genuinely want to help patients. They are concerned when anything goes wrong, with or without fault, and courtrooms perceive this commitment through all the intrigue and rancor associated with most hearings. Nevertheless, preparation may not equal serendipity, but it adds insurance.

In preparing anyone for public speaking, a television appearance, or an acting assignment, the crucial element is to simulate the foreign environment into which the performer will be thrust. It is unlikely that a lawyer will set up a mock courtroom in which the physician can rehearse, but some efforts in this direction will prove rewarding. In most trials the physician is going to have to face the "prosecutor" before he has a chance to relate his own story. If the lawyer anticipates the plaintiff's arguments, he should prepare the doctor by putting him in a chair in the corner, walking back twenty feet and roaring away. He should ask tough, embarrassing questions, roll out the skeletons and even throw in a few low punches. This is the time for the demeanor to be polished. Not since residency has this physician had to endure harsh criticism of his professional opinions, and a little review is highly desirable. The more skilled the lawyer is in anticipating the plaintiff's plan of attack, the better he or she is able to assist his client. In a major case where the physician is truly inexperienced and not responding to this "Dale Carnegie" approach, the lawyer should consider finding an empty courtroom and creating a session in the real environment. Where applicable, consider the use of a video to obtain maximum preparation. This can pay significant dividends. In summary, put the client through a mock direct and cross-examination.

A final caveat which the legal profession must address is peculiar to the large metropolitan malpractice defense firms. Traditionally, the physician is handed up the ladder of seniority as the case progresses. Unfortunately, this negates most of what has been said in developing a comfortable doctor-lawyer relationship. The doctor is continually dealing with new players in a situation which is basically foreign. Perhaps there is no agreeable solution to this problem in a large specialty firm. However, one thought is to have the junior associate who first met the doctor, and has become a confidant, continue to be present during the final sessions. This will provide a semblance of continuity to this delicate partnership.

In summary, the entire thrust of this chapter can be distilled down to one single concept. The lawyer must get to know his client early in the suit and communicate. He or she must be available outside the nine-to-five routine and avoid the all too common night-before preparation. While upholding the legalities of a malpractice suit, the lawyer must be aware of the doctor's perspective throughout the case. In doing so the lawyer will not only win more cases, but be more effective in those that are lost. The result will satisfy the finest attributes of the legal profession.

CHAPTER FIVE

A PSYCHOTHERAPIST'S DUTY TO WARN AN INTENDED VICTIM OF THE THREAT OF HARM FROM A PATIENT

John R. Marshall, Jr., Esq.

I. INTRODUCTION

In September 1973 Norman Madsen stabbed his father to death at their home with a knife.

This fatal incident was preceded by the son having years of drug abuse and periodic psychiatric hospitalizations from June 1969 through January 1973. The hospital history shows the patient's hostility and anger toward his parents and particular hatred for his father. The patient was released on community out-patient status from January 1973 to June 1973 when he was discharged.

In October 1972, while hospitalized, the patient, during a psychotic episode, expressed the ideation he would "like" to kill his father by stabbing him in the heart but actually only "like" to stab him in the stomach. This threat was never again repeated by the patient. In the meantime, seven months elapsed until discharge and almost one year until the killing without the threat of killing being repeated and the patient making satisfactory progress in his mental condition.

This history of the patient, the threat to kill and death of the father was the basis for a claim being filed against the State of New York. *Helen L. Madsen, as Administratrix of the Estate of Norman O. Madsen, Deceased v. The State of New York*, Claim No. 59538.

Following a bifurcated trial, Court of Claims Judge Jerome F. Hanifin rendered a decision on the issue of liability only dated March 17, 1982. The decision was entered March 22, 1982 (claimant has appealed and the appeal is still pending). The Court of Claims decision is unreported.

The Court noted there was no claim made for negligent release of the patient and opined the evidence, in any event, was lacking on such an issue.

The claim was based on three theories: (1) negligent diagnosis, (2) negligent supervision, and (3) state doctor's failure to warn father of the October 1972 psychotic episode killing ideation. This third issue is the subject matter of this chapter. The Court rejected the first two claims, found there was no duty to warn under the circumstances and found the decedent guilty of contributory negligence. Accordingly, the claim was dismissed.

The duty of a therapist to warn an intended victim of harm threatened by a patient is an issue of first impression in New York State.

II. BASIS OF A DUTY TO WARN

Claimant Madsen contended the Court should find a duty to warn and apply to this case the California case of first impression. *Tarasoff v. Regents of University of California*, 551 P.2d 334 (1976); *see also McIntosh v. Milano*, 403 A.2d 500 (1979, N.J.).

The *Tarasoff* case argued its way to defining the duty by eliminating the four fundamental arguments used by those opposing the recognition of such a duty: (1) violation of the doctor-patient privilege. No violation since the duty to warn is an exception to the privilege and due to section 9 of the Principles of Medical Ethics of the American Medical Association allowing a doctor to reveal a patient's confidence ". . . to protect the welfare of the individual or of the community." The *Madsen* decision agrees with *Tarasoff* that this medical ethic applies to mental disease as well as physical contagious diseases. The exception is justified only when warning is necessary to avert danger to others since the protective privilege ends where the public peril begins, *Tarasoff, supra*; (2) impractical to implement the duty since it is next to impossible to predict dangerousness or future dangerous acts by a mental patient. As a practical matter, doctors do this every day in courtrooms in applying various laws to mental patients, i.e., admission to hospitals, retention hearings and C.P.L. sec. 330.20 hearings; (3) aggravate an existing tendency of therapists to overpredict dangerousness resulting in the unnecessary commitment of mental patients; and (4) seriously impair the psychotherapeutic process.

Once the legal and medical arguments against such a duty were eliminated, the *Tarasoff* case stated the legal basis for this new duty as applied to therapists of mental patients. The basis for the new duty is founded on section 315, Restatement of the Law of Torts, 1st and 2nd Editions:

> There is no duty so to curtail the conduct of a third person as to prevent him from causing bodily harm to another unless, (a) a special relation exists between the actor and the third person which imposes a duty upon the actor to curtail the third person's conduct, or (b) a special relation exists between the actor and the other which gives to the other a right to protection.

Tarasoff imposes this new duty to warn on a therapist where a special relationship exists between him and his patient. The doctor-patient relation creates the special relationship. This special relationship creates a duty for a therapist to control his patient. The definition of the duty, when it exists, establishes the control standards. *See also McIntosh, supra*, on the basis for the new duty.

III. DEFINITION OF THE DUTY TO WARN

Tarasoff at 551 P.2d 334, 340 defined the duty as follows:

> When a therapist determines, or pursuant to the standards of his profession should determine that his patient presents a serious danger of violence to another, he incurs an obligation to us reasonable care to protect the intended victim against such danger. The discharge of this duty may require the thereapist to take one or more of various steps, depending upon the nature of the case. Thus, it may call for him to warn the intended victim or others likely to appraise the victim of the danger, to notify the police, or to take whatever other steps are reasonably necessary under the circumstances.

Other cases recognizing the duty to warn are: (1) *McIntosh, supra;* (2) *Dept. of Health and Rehabilitation Serv. v. McDougall,* 359 So.2d 528 (Fla., 1978); (3) *Lipari v. Sears, Roebuck and Co.*, 497 F. Supp. 185 (Neb., 1980); (4) *Leedy v. Hartnet,* 510 F. Supp. 1125 (Pa., 1981); (5) *Merchants National Bank and Trust Co. of Fargo v. U.S.*, 272 F. Supp. 409 (N.D., 1967); (6) *The Bradley Center, Inc. v. Wessner,* 287 S.E.2d 716 (Ga., 1982); (7) *Mavroudis v. Superior Ct. of San Mateo County,* 162 Cal. Rptr. 724 (Calif., 1980); (8) *Thompson v. Co. of Alameda,* 152 Cal. Rptr. 226 (1979), *aff'd,* 167 Cal. Rptr. 70, *aff'd complaint dismissal,* 614 P.2d 728 (1980, Supreme Court of Calif.). The California Supreme Court vacated the opinion reported at 152 Cal. Rptr. 226.

IV. APPLICATION OF THE DUTY TO WARN

The *Madsen* decision had " . . . no reservations recognizing the existence of a special relationship between a therapist and a patient which may give rise to a duty on the part of the thereapist to take steps to protect a third person. The factual circumstances which precipitate such duty, however, must be extreme and the serious danger perceived must be truly immediate." *Id.* at 39; *see also McIntosh, supra.* Therefore, the duty is not broad based but is a limited duty. *See Mavroudis, supra.* Limiting the duty recognizes the extent of the doctor-patient privilege, the difficulty doctors encounter in determining current or future dangerousness, and possibly reduce the tendency to overpredict dangerousness. In *Madsen* the circumstances were not extreme since the patient was in the controlled environment of the hospital and only mentioned he would "like" to kill his father one time during a psychotic episode. Also the danger perceived was not immediate since the killing ideation did not continue, most of the last hospital stay was unremarkable and the Court agreed that the state doctor had not other choice but to release the patient pursuant to law. The *Madsen* decision found no duty to warn as a matter of law even uder the *Tarasoff* decision. The *Madsen* decision noted the *Tarasoff* threat was immediate, the patient was promptly released after admission, the therapist believed the patient was dangerous since he notified the police of the patient's release from the hospital and the patient said he intended to kill his victim whereas *Madsen* only said he would "like" to kill his father. In *Tarasoff* the doctor determined the patient was a danger. In *Madsen* the doctor determined to release the patient months later since he was no longer a danger.

The victim of the threat must be readily identifiable. A specific victim need not be known. It may be unreasonable to require a doctor to question the patient or to conduct an additional investigation to determine the victim's identity. A moment's reflection by the doctor may reveal the victim's identity. The matter depends on the circumstances of each case. There can't be any hard and fast rule. *Tarasoff*, 551 P.2d 334. *See also Thompson, supra; Merchants National Bank, supra*; *Mavroudis, supra*; *Doyle v. U.S.*, 530 F. Supp. 1278 (Calif., 1982). That a doctor may be inaccurate in predicting dangerousness does not negate the existence of the duty. *See Tarasoff, supra*; *Lipari, supra*.

For the duty to apply the doctor must know to whom to give the warning. Where a patient had known violent tendencies when drinking but made no threats against his victim and no evidence he was more prone to be violent toward people in whose presence he was comfortable, there was no duty to warn people with whom he would have social contact. This patient assaulted a friend with whom he resided after hospital discharge. *Leedy, supra*.

The duty to warn does not exist where a warning would not guard against the risk. A patient in a State veteran's home was allowed to drive his car on a pass from the home even though the home knew he was on medication and his driving was risky to others. The patient was involved in a two-car fatal accident. *Harland v. State*, 142 Cal. Rptr. 201 (Calif., 1977). *See also Thompson*, *supra*, where no duty to warn existed since the actor (known to be violent) made nonspecific threats (kill a boy in his neighborhood) directed at nonspecific victims. Warning a broad segment of the population could only be general in nature and difficult to give. Also not required was notice to the police since there would be no guarantee the police would transmit the notice to potential victims.

Also see the following cases:

1. *State v. Tarbutton*, 407 A.2d 538 (Del., 1979). Discusses the potential liability of a doctor who testifies in a defendant release hearing after defendant acquitted by insanity where the court releases defendant to the community and defendant harms a victim.

2. *Shaw v. Glickman*, 415 A.2d 625 (Md., 1980). Where a doctor was treating a husband, wife and the wife's lover, no duty to warn even though the husband shot the lover while in bed with the wife. The doctor was not told of any threats to harm the lover and couldn't infer any threat to harm from the doctor's knowledge that the husband carried a gun.

3. *Cole v. Taylor*, 301 N.W.2d 766 (Iowa, 1981). A patient who killed a person can't sue her treating doctor for a failure to warn the victim. Pursuant to *Tarasoff*, the duty to warn runs to the victim and not to the patient.

Even though a duty to warn exists, the facts and circumstances of a given case may allow a finding there was, as a matter of law, no duty to warn. This argument is important particularly in a case like *Madsen* where the court factually determined the state doctor gave no warning. The following facts and circumstances should be considered: (1) patient's entire history; (2) family or victim's knowledge of patient's violent propensities; (3) circumstances under which the threat is made and the language used to express the threat; (4) time lapse between the threat and infliction of harm on the victim; (5) did a special relationship exist between the doctor and patient; (6) was a warning given even if not required; (7) circumstances surrounding the warning and how warning was given—was it recorded in the hospital record; (8) did the therapist actually determine dangerousness; (9) should dangerousness have been determined pursuant to professional standards; (10) nature of the threat—was it specific or nonspecific; (11) was the victim at least readily identifiable; (12)

relationship between the patient and victim from hospital release or discharge to date of harm; (13) was any failure to warn the proximate cause of the harm to the victim; (14) was the victim guilty of any culpable conduct such as contributory negligence.

V. VICTIM'S CONTRIBUTORY NEGLIGENCE

The victim being threatened by the patient on a prior occasion is immaterial to the applicability of the duty to warn, but is a factual defense. *See McIntosh, supra*; *see also Madsen* decision, *Id.* at 46. The *Madsen* decision found the decedent father to be guilty of contributory negligence. Contributory negligence applied to this case and not the later doctrine of comparative negligence. The case result probably would have been the same even applying the doctrine of comparative negligence.

From October 1972 (when the threat was made) through release on community status and until discharge and until shortly before the fatal event, the son only felt he had failed his father. But the chilling events preceeding the father's death by hours made the father realize the risk his son posed.

A sister complained she had been sexually accosted by her brother Norman Madsen. The father approached the house with a hatchet under his coat. The son was acting in a bizarre fashion. The son threatened to kill his father with a hammer, gun and screwdriver. One month before the fatal events a sister wrote a letter to a friend expressing a fear that her brother was going to try to kill her or her father soon. After the father observed his son in a dangerous state, the Vestal police arrived and offered to take the son to the state hosptial. The final events were set in motion when the father and mother both refused the offer of the police. Shortly after the police left, the son stabbed his father to death in their home. "Since Mr. Madsen observed Norman in a dangerous state prior to the arrival of the police and failed to have Norman recommitted, he must at least share in the responsibility for what ultimately occurred." *Madsen Id.* at 48.

The duty to warn is not absolute and the victim's culpable conduct may mitigate the amount of damages or deny recovery.

SELECTED RESOURCE CITATIONS

1. Note, *Imposing a Duty on Psychiatrists—A Judicial Threat to the Psychiatric Profession,* 48 U. Colo. L. Rev. 283, 287 n. 26, 298-299 (1977).

2. Stone, *The* Tarasoff *Decisions: Suing Psychiatrists to Safeguard Society,* 90 Harv. L. Rev. 358 (1976).

3. Fleming and Maximar, *The Patient or His Victim: The Therapist's Dilemma*, 62 Calif. L. Rev. 1025 (1974).

4. Comment, Tarasoff *and the Psychotherapist's Duty to Warn*, 12 San Diego L. Rev. 932 (1975).

5. Note, Tarasoff v. Regents of the U. Calif. *The Duty to Warn: Common Law and Statutory Problems for Calif. Psychotherapists*, 14 Cal. Western L. Rev. 153 (1978-79).

6. Note, *Untangling* Tarasoff: Tarasoff v. Regents of the U. of Calif., 29 Hastings L.J. 179 (1977-78).

7. Comment, *Discovery of Psychotherapist-Patient Communications after* Tarasoff. (Contains cites to additional articles on *Tarasoff* subject matter.) 15 San Diego L. Rev. 265.

8. *Legal Duty to Warn Potential Victims*, 9 Akron L. Rev. 191 (Summer—'75).

9. *Duty to Warn Potential Victims*, 6 Seton Hall 536 (Spring—1975).

10. *Duty to Warn Victim*, 44 U. Cin. L. Rev. 368 (1975).

11. *The Psychotherapists Peril*, 37 U. Pitt. L. Rev. 155 (Fall—1975).

12. *Duty to Warn Victim*, 28 Vand. L. Rev. 631 (April—1975).

13. *Application of the* Tarasoff *Duty to Forensic Psychiatry*, 66 Va L. Rev. 715 (April—1980).

14. *Tort Law—Duty to Warn— Psychiatrist's Duty to Warn Third Parties of Dangerous Patients,* 19 Duq. L. Rev. 181 (Fall—1980).

15. *Liability of One Treating Mentally Afflicted Patient for Failure to Warn or Protect Third Persons Threatened by Patient,* 83 A.L.R. 3rd 1201 (see p. 1205 for citations to law review articles).

16. Gurevity, Tarasoff *Protective Privilege Versus Public Peril,* 134 Am. J. Psych. 289, 291 (1977).

17. Roth and Meisel, *Dangerousness, Confidentiality, and the Duty to Warn,* 134 Am. J. Psych. 508 (1977).

CHAPTER SIX

THE MALPRACTICE PANEL—PLAINTIFF

Fred Peters, Esq.

I. IN GENERAL

The preparation of material for consideration by the panel members varies with the jurisdiction involved. Some require simple letters; others prefer medical briefs.

Preparation of a medical brief is the most comprehensive form of submission. Preferably, the brief should commence with a statement of facts which should include all pertinent background material, such as:

1. Age of the plaintiff;

2. Identities of all parties;

3. Alleged roles of the defendants in the medical treatment;

4. The sequence of events (in narrative form);

5. A description of the injury and disability.

After the statements of facts, each allegation of malpractice or departure from accepted medical practice should be captioned as a Point. Following the caption, a discussion of the basis for the allegation and Point and general description of the medical conduct should be discussed.

Where possible, corroboration of Points should be made with reference to actual testimony adduced at the examination before trial. Such testimony should be excerpted, giving reference to page and line numbers as they appear in the deposition itself. It is necessary to include with the presentation the following:

1. Copies of all hospital records which are illustrative of the Points alleged;

2. Copies of any Medical Journal articles or text book excerpts, with appropriate reference information;

3. It may be advisable to include copies of expert's report and opinion. Caution should be taken to delete the name and address from such report, but information should be given as to the specialty of the physician expert.

The use of an expert's report may be omitted.

Objections to proposed panel members should be made immediately upon being notified as to their identity by the court. Any delay will be fatal to such objections.

The following steps should be taken when identity of the panel expert is received with respect to the medical panelist:

1. Has he been sued in a medical malpractice action?

2. Is he regularly employed as an expert by the defense?

3. Do you have any cases pending against him?

4. Is he associated with any hospitals in common with one or more of the defendants?

5. Does he have the proper specialty?

If any information is developed, it should be communicated to the court in a letter of objections. With respect to the attorney panelist:

1. Is he regularly a defendant's lawyer?

2. Does he have any connection with an insurance company?

3. Does he represent hospitals or physicians in other types of legal matters?

4. Have you ever been in opposition to him in any litigation?

II. CONDUCTING THE PANEL HEARING ITSELF

At the hearing, the allegations of medical malpractice should be stated succinctly, together with the salient features of the medical care upon which you rely.

Every attempt should be made to express your arguments in a fair manner, avoiding the use of inflammatory language.

Any questions put by the panel members should be answered directly and forthrightly.

The presentation made by your adversaries should be carefully noted in order to ascertain the direction of their defense.

III. SIGNIFICANCE AT TRIAL OF THE PANEL HEARING

1. If there has been a unanimous finding of liability, reference to this should be reserved until opening, and not on jury selection.

2. If there has been a unanimous finding of no liability, it is imperative to discuss it during jury selection.

3. A decision must be made whether to subpoena the medical or legal panelist for the trial. This can play an important role in convincing the jury that the finding was not justified, if it is against your case.

4. If there is no unanimous finding, then no reference to a panel hearing may be made whatsoever.

(A specimen form of panel brief is annexed.)

ANNEX—SPECIMEN FORM OF PANEL BRIEF

PLAINTIFF'S STATEMENT OF FACTS RE: MEDICAL MALPRACTICE PANEL

The deceased herein was 46 years of age and was admitted to the Central General Hospital on April 30, 1978, by his physician, Dr. Melvin Holden, because of suspicious chest pains.

Dr. Holden is a Board certified specialist in internal medicine and was the treating physician during the hospital admission.

After admission and after further EKGs were performed, the patient was transferred to the Cardiac Care Unit of the hospital under Dr. Holden's care, where he remained until May 7, 1978, a period of approximately five days.

Dr. Holden consulted with Dr. Abraham Azulay who was the Chief of Cardiology at the hospital. Dr. Azulay is not certified in cardiology. Dr. Azulay saw the patient daily while he was in the Cardiac Care Unit and participated in his diagnosis and treatment with Dr. Holden.

During the early afternoon of May 7 the patient was transferred from the Cardiac Care Unit to a general care floor in the hospital by Dr. Holden.

Approximately ten hours later the patient had a cardiac arrest and expired following an episode of dysrhythmia.

It is contended herein that the defendants departed from good and accepted medical practice respectively in four main areas. They will be discussed in the order in which they occurred and not in the order of their importance.

1.

THE PHYSICIANS PREMATURELY DISCONTINUED AN ANTI-ARRHYTHMIA DRUG AND SUBSTITUTED A LESS EFFECTIVE ONE.

A diagnosis was made, by reason of the electrocardiographic findings on May 1, 1978, that the patient had suffered an anterior transmural myocardial infarction, which is certainly a moderate or moderately severe type of infarction.

Because the patient, while in the Cardiac Care Unit, was experiencing episodes of dysrhythmia in the form of premature ventricular contractions and had a run of bigeminal rhythm, the physicians prescribed Lidocaine (Xylocaine) to be administered I.V. (see hospital record).

On May 2, 1978, despite the Lidocaine, an episode of ventricular fibrillation occurred following a PVC on T wave. He was successfully electrically defibrillated and the dose of Lidocaine was increased to 4 mcg. a minute.

X-rays showed the formation of cardiomegaly and pulmonary vascular congestion. Rhonchi and rales bilaterally were noted and the patient became febrile. An additional diagnosis of congestive heart failure and pericarditis, together with hypotension, was made on May 2nd.

On May 3rd a note in the record indicates that an S-4 gallop rhythm was detected, from which Dr. Holden concluded that the pulmonary congestion was increasing.

On May 3rd, according to the testimony by Dr. Holden, because of a finding of rales in both lung bases he felt that more fluid had accumulated in the lungs than the previous day and for this he prescribed a diuretic.

The prescription for Xylocaine was reduced to 3½ mcg. per minute. A sputum culture and sensitivity for possible lung infection was ordered on May 3rd. This order was never carried out by the hospital.

Following the reduction in Xylocaine on May 4th, the patient had additional dysrhythmias in the form of PVCs and, according to the record, an extra bolus of Xylocaine was administered by the nurse in the Cardiac Care Unit because of the onset of two PVCs in a row.

On May 5th the patient still had fluid in the lungs.

On May 5th Dr. Holden made an order to discontinue the Lidocaine at 1:00 p.m. and to commence giving the patient Norpace by mouth: 150 mg. at 1:30 p.m., 150 mg. at 3:00 p.m. and at 6:00 p.m. to begin giving 150 mg. every six hours.

The avowed purpose of administering both the Xylocaine and the Norpace was to minimize and, if possible, to avoid the onset of dysrhythmia, which is potentially a life-threatening problem in this type of patient.

Unquestionably, Lidocaine is the more effective drug for this purpose and is considered the drug of choice. One of the reasons for this is the ease with which it is administered and the fact that it can be administered I.V., a route which provides for more rapid use by the body.

Norpace, on the other hand, is administered by mouth and is therefore absorbed more slowly and is considered to be somewhat less effective.

This patient, who demonstrated a recurrence of dysrhythmias following a small reduction in Xylocaine, it is respectfully submitted, should not have been changed to Norpace without sufficient reason existing. The only reason given by Dr. Holden for changing the medication to Norpace was because he considered that the Xylocaine was responsible for the onset of neurolgical side effects. He testified as follows:

DR. HOLDEN E.B.T.

PAGE 148, LINE 14, *ET SEQ.*:

Q: Specifically, what was the reason for wanting to change medication?

A: I was afraid that the patient was demonstrating neurologic symptoms from too excessive Xylocaine levels.

Q: What symptoms specifically had you noted?

A: He was restless or edgy, as I state here.

Q: Anything else?

A: No.

There is no indication whatever in the chart that any neurological side effects whatsoever were being produced by the Xylocaine.

As a matter of fact, Dr. Azulay, during his deposition, acknowledged that there were in fact no side effects being produced by the Xylocaine.

DR. AZULAY E.B.T.

PAGE 44, LINE 7, *ET SEQ.*:

Q: Now, sir, with regard to particularly this patient, did this patient, to your knowledge, develop any side effects from Xylocaine?

A: No. I specifically noted that in the record that he did not.

Thus, it appears that the drug of choice was discontinued and another drug utilized, without sufficient reason.

It is also interesting and important to note that these drugs must be administered in such a fashion so as to take into consideration the half-life, and in such a manner so as to insure that the desired blood level be maintained.

Additionally, according to the manufacturer's package insert for Norpace, a warning is issued that it may cause or worsen congestive heart failure and produce severe hypotension. It is not recommended for use in patients with such conditions. Furthermore, when Norpace is to be used in cardiac patients who are hospitalized, and for the purpose of suppressing dysrhythmias, such a patient is to be monitored closely.

The patient was transferred from the Cardiac Care Unit on May 7th with an order to be given the Norpace by general care nurses on the regular floor, every six hours. In other words, to continue the regimen of treatment started in the Cardiac Care Unit, despite the fact that appropriate monitoring facilities did not exist anywhere in the hospital, except in the Cardiac Care Unit.

2.

IN LIGHT OF THE PATIENT'S CONDITION AND THE NEED FOR CONTINUED ELECTRONIC MONITORING OR OBSERVATION BY SPECIALLY TRAINED PERSONNEL, HE WAS PREMATURELY TRANSFERRED FROM THE CARDIAC CARE UNIT TO THE GENERAL CARE WARD.

According to the hospital record, the patient was placed in the Cardiac Care Unit on May 1st, during which time serial electrocardiograms were performed, which confirmed a diagnosis of transmural myocardial infarction; the patient complained of increasing chest pain and had "a run of bigeminal rhythm" and he was given anti-arrhythmia medication and Demarol for pain; and he was also noted to have developed a gallop rhythm.

The next day, on May 2nd, he had a life-threatening episode of ventricular fibrillation which required electric shock for defibrillation. Increased doses of anti-arrhythmia medication, together with Inderal and Nitropaste were administered and he was also given Heparin. Later on the same day, he complained of retrosternal pain and a friction rub, and developed hypotension.

On the next day, May 3rd, laboratory enzyme reports showed a marked elevation of CPK, greater than 1500, with a 22% MB or type 2 (cardiac type).

He became febrile and developed lung congestion, indicative of congestive heart failure, for which he was given Lasix.

By May 2nd, electrocardiographic changes were noted, some of which were indicative as evidence of pericarditis having developed. For instance, there was increased Q wave and further loss of R wave in the left upper anterior frontal area of LVL-L1. The lack of R wave appeared to extend from V4R through V4L in a 17 lead cardiogram, with an abnormal low R and V5. There was an increase in the ST elevation and prolongation of the T wave compared to a previous hyperacute short T wave.

Dr. Azulay has testified that another EKG was taken on May 4th which indicated no changes, but that the electrocardiogram taken on May 6th indicated "no definite significant change." He attributed some minimal variations in possible differences in placement of the electrodes. Thus, on May

6th, the patient was in essentially the same clinical condition, according to the EKG interpreted by defendant Dr. Azulay, as he had been for the previous three days.

Dr. Holden has testified that the lung congestion and fluid were increasing on May 3rd. He further testified that on May 4th arrhythmias were detected and the patient had to be given the extra Xylocaine mentioned hereinabove.

Dr. Holden has conceded in his deposition that the occurrence of premature ventricular contractions, as they took place on May 4th, may be a harbinger, if untreated, of a serious life-threatening problem.

DR. HOLDEN E.B.T.

PAGE 143, LINE 22, *ET SEQ.*:

Q: Does the fact that two PVCs in a row occur mean anything?

A: Well, that it should be treated to avoid—two in a row should be treated to avoid ventricular fibrillations.

Q: In other words, may that be a harbinger, if untreated, of a more serious life-threatening problem?

A: Yes.

The patient's lung congestion was still present on May 5th and he still was running a fever.

On May 5th multiple PVCs were recorded by the nurses in the Cardiac Care Unit, according to the record and the testimony of Dr. Azulay.

DR. AZULAY E.B.T.

PAGE 91, LINE 23, *ET SEQ.*:

Q: Doctor, would you tell me please if, on May 5th, there is an indication in the Nurses' Notes that there were multiple PVCs recorded on that day?

A: On May 5th, there was—there were multiple PVCs recorded.

Some time on May 6th a decision was made to transfer the patient from the Cardiac Care Unit to the general floor care. This decision was implemented by transfer during the early afternoon of May 7th.

This transfer was made despite the following circumstances which are recorded in the record and conceded on deposition:

1) A cardiogram taken on May 6th exhibits changes in the precordial leads, which are strongly suggestive of recrudesence or extension of the myocardial infarction;

2) The patient was suffering from hypotension;

3) The patient was suffering from congestive heart failure;

4) The patient had a fever of 101.6;

5) The patient experienced PVCs while on Lidocaine therapy;

6) The medication had been changed to Norpace which had been given for only one day, without adequate documentation as to his response to this change in medication.

Thus, the patient was transferred to an environment where he would not receive the benefits of continuous electrocardiographic monitoring and observation by specially trained personnel, and at a time when the doctors could not be reasonably sure that the Norpace would have the desired effect in suppressing arrhythmias.

As a patient on the general floor commencing in the early afternoon of May 7th, he was never again seen by any physican prior to his death. Moreover, he was observed by the floor nurse on few occasions merely for the purpose of recording his vital signs, and even these were not properly charted in that the pulse rate was omitted from their recorded observations.

The defendants have conceded that the patient, undoubtedly, suffered an episode of dysrhythmia which progressed to ventricular fibrillation, and resulted in his death at a time when no one was observing him, except for a nurse's visit a few moments prior thereto. The conduct of the nurse on that occasion will be commented upon below.

3.

THERE WAS AN INEXCUSABLE DEPARTURE FROM GOOD HOSPITAL AND NURSING PRACTICE IN THE FAILURE TO ADMINISTER THE ANTI-ARRHYTHMIC DRUG, NORPACE, TO THE PATIENT AS ORDERED BY HIS PHYSICIAN.

The record indicates, and Doctors Azulay and Holden have both testified unequivocally, Xylocaine was discontinued on May 5th, and instead Norpace was used. It was the intention of the physicians to have the patient take that medication in sufficient doses and sufficient frequency to maintain an optimum blood level of the drug in order to suppress the advent of dysrhythmia. Defendants acknowledge that dysrhythmia may be life threatening.

Clearly, the record indicates that beginning at 6:00 p.m. on May 5th, the patient was ordered to be given Norpace; 150 mg. of Norpace every six hours, after having already received a total of 300 mg. divided by two separate doses earlier that afternoon.

When the patient was transferred from the Cardiac Care Unit on May 7th, Dr. Holden repeated the written order directing the nurses on the floor to continue administering Norpace every six hours in the same dosage.

Unquestionably, the proper administration of this medication requires that its half-life be considered and that repetition of dosage must be maintained in order to maintain the therapeutic level in the blood. It was vital for this patient's well-being, in connection with the possibility of dysrhythmia, for him to have this medication given as ordered. The order required him to receive the medication for the last time in the Cardiac Care Unit at 12 noon on May 7th, and thereafter to receive it at 6:00 p.m. and midnight, after his transfer to the general floor.

A careful examination of the hospital record indicates that the last dose of Norpace that this patient received before his death was the one given to him at 12 noon in the Cardiac Care Unit.

It was the practice in this hospital for medication orders to be recorded on a Kardex file for use by the medication and charge nurse on the floor. It is conceded that the Kardex contained information concerning Dr. Holden's written order for Norpace, and that it indicated that the patient was to receive it at 6:00 p.m. and at midnight on May 7th.

Inexplicably, the nurses who were on duty on the ward to which the patient had been transferred neglected to follow the doctor's order with respect to the 6:00 p.m. Norpace medication, and the patient never received it.

It was at approximately 11:40 p.m. on that date that the nurse, then on duty, visited the patient for the purpose of taking his vital signs preparatory to giving him his midnight medication. The patient, unfortunately, within a few minutes, suffered the dysrhythmia for which the medication had been prescribed and not given, and expired of cardiac arrest secondary thereto, a few minutes later. He never received his medication after 12 noon, approximately 12 hours prior to his death.

Obviously, this act of neglect on the part of the nursing staff resulted in the therapeutic levels in the patient's blood being less than the physician desired, with tragic consequence.

Dr. Holden and Dr. Azulay both testified at their depositions that the order for Norpace, as written in the record, was never countermanded by any physician, and it was mandatory for the nurses to have followed it. The nurses had no authorization to omit the 6:00 p.m. medication; and they further have testified that it was a departure form good and accepted practice not to have followed the physician's orders.

DR. HOLDEN E.B.T.

PAGE 159, LINE 21, *ET SEQ.*:

Q: If it was not given, was it a departure from good and accepted practice, nursing practice, if failed to be given in view of the outstanding order?

A: I would answer that yes.

The importance of this neglect is further highlighted by Dr. Holden's testimony as follows:

DR. HOLDEN E.B.T.

PAGE 160, LINE 6, *ET SEQ.*:

Q: And would the absence of Norpace between 12 noon on May 7th and midnight or approximately on the same day or a period of twelve hours have a deleterious effect, in your opinion, on his condition?

A: It's a possibility.

At the very least, one must conclude that the failure to give the patient the medication deemed necessary by his physician deprived the patient of the only medical means available to deal with dysrhythmias.

4.

THE FAILURE ON THE PART OF THE NURSE TO TAKE IMMEDIATE ACTION, WHEN SHE DISCOVERED THE PATIENT'S BLOOD PRESSURE HAD DROPPED, RESULTED IN A DELAY IN RESUSCITATIVE MEASURES BEING TAKEN, AND DEPRIVED THE DECEASED OF AN OPPORTUNITY TO SURVIVE.

After having been placed on the general floor, the patient was observed by the nursing staff on relatively few occasions, as indicated by the hospital record.

At approximately 11:50 p.m., the nursing record indicates that the patient stated that he was "sweating" and wanted to change his gown. At that time, the nurse took the blood pressure in preparation for giving him his midnight medication of Norpace, and found him to have a blood pressure of 70/50. Accordingly, the nurse decided to withhold the Norpace, returned to the nursing station, leaving the patient alone, and had a conversation with the charge nurse concerning the blood pressure finding. She then decided to return and retake the blood pressure. She also obtained a fresh gown for the patient because his sweating resulted in his gown becoming wet. When she returned to the patient's room, which she records as three minutes later, she found the patient unresponsive, without respiration, looking blue, and she called for help.

A resuscitation team responded. He was defibrillated five times, but the patient arrested and expired.

The above episode is fully described in those terms by the testimony of Nurse Brennan in her deposition, and she is the nurse who found the blood pressure to be 70/50. She was aware that the patient was a coronary patient and had recently suffered a myocardial infarction, and was aware that he was on anti-arrhythmia medication.

NURSE BRENNAN E.B.T.

PAGE 32, LINE 20, *ET SEQ.*:

Q: Were you advised at any time prior to the time you went into Mr. Kanfer's room that he was a coronary patient?

A: Yes.

PAGE 37, LINE 7, *ET SEQ.*:

Q: And can you tell me what his blood pressure was, or you can refresh your recollection if you want from the record.

A: 70 over 50.

PAGE 38, LINE 6, *ET SEQ.*:

Q: And when you first went into the room at 11:50, other than observing the patient and taking his blood pressure, did you do anything else?

A: I don't recall.

Q: Did you have any conversation with the patient with regard to his perspiring, at that time?

A: Let me see. I noticed he was perspiring. He said he was sweaty and I said, "Okay, I will get you another gown."

Q: And either after or before taking the blood pressure, did you take Mr. Kanfer's pulse, at that particular time, 11:50?

A: I took the blood pressure and it was low so I went straight outside to the nurse to find out what his blood pressure usually is in his condition, at the time.

PAGE 40, LINE 6, *ET SEQ.*:

Q: I think you testified thereupon you left that room. Can you tell me where you went when you left his room after taking the blood pressure?

A: I went immediately into the nursing station to find out what his normal vital signs were and then I returned right after I found out.

Q: And what were his normal vital signs?

A: I don't recall.

PAGE 42, LINE 7, *ET SEQ.*:

Q: Did you have any conversation with Nurse Monten after leaving the patient's room and after you took his blood pressure, with regard to what this patient's normal blood pressure should have been?

A: Yes.

Q: Do you recall the substance of that conversation?

A: I told her that Mr. Kanfer's blood pressure was 70 over 50 and what is his normal. She looked it up on the blood pressure sheet and I returned to his room.

Q: Did she say anything to you after she looked it up on the blood pressure sheet?

A: "Check his blood pressure again."

PAGE 44, LINE 22, *ET SEQ.*:

Q: When you went back to his room for the second time, you stated that there was no verbal response. Can you tell me what you observed with your eyes with regard to his physical condition, if anything?

A: He was just laying there.

Q: Did you observe his coloring?

A: It was poor, cyanotic.

Q: Would that be pale?

A: Blue.

Q: Did you observe whether he was perspiring or sweating?

A: At that time, no, he was not.

Q: And are those all of the observations that you recall at this time when you entered his room for the second time or what you visualized is all?

A: He was unresponsive and that's really all that mattered, at that point.

Q: Upon seeing that he was unresponsive, what did you then do, if anything?

A: Called the cardiac arrest from his bed. I was at his bed.

Further comment on this testimony would be superfluous.

CONCLUSION

A combination of departures from both accepted medical practice and accepted hospital and nursing care resulted in the patient's losing whatever chance he had of recovering and surviving a serious myocardial infarction.

CHAPTER SEVEN

MEDICAL MALPRACTICE PANEL: BENEFIT OR BURDEN—RECENT CONSIDERATIONS

John P. LoPresti, Jr., Esq.

I. PREFACE

No other recent piece of legislation in tort law has caused more controversy, confusion and dissatisfaction on the part of plaintiffs and defendants alike than has the enactment of Judiciary Law sec. 148-a, which established the Medical Malpractice Panel in cases in which physicians and/or hospitals are sued. There is virtual unanimity of opinion in both camps that the Panel is just not accomplishing that purpose for which it was conceived, i.e., to expedite the course and ultimate resolution of claims brought against physicians and hospitals by discouraging frivolous claims and by providing an impetus for the settlement of valid ones. Indeed, there is nothing expeditious about the handling and resolution of medical malpractice cases. A considerable number of these actions (especially those venued within the counties of the city of New York) are the oldest cases on the calendar. A number of reasons could be ascribed to this fact, but more often than not, the cases have not been tried because they are awaiting a hearing and determination before a Medical Malpractice Panel.

II. THE STATUTE

Section 148-a of the Judiciary Law makes provision for the establishment of a panel to facilitate the disposition of medical malpractice claims. In essence, as originally enacted in 1974, the statute provides for the following procedures:

> All hearings are held before a panel of three members, consisting of a Justice of the Supreme Court, a physician and an attorney (subd. 2)[n] The panel doctor and attorney are selected from a list prepared by the Presiding Justice of each respective Appellate Division (subd. 2, pars. (a), (b)). The listing of doctors is by specialty as is determined and communicated to the court by the Medical Society of the State of New York, a county medical society and/or the New York Academy of Medicine; attorneys selected are required to have trial experience, not confined, however, to the field of medical malpractice (subd. 2, pars. (a), (b)).

[n]The panel may request "an additional doctor having particular expertise in the specialty involved to assist in the determination of the claim." (subd. 6)

> Prior to the date set for the hearing any party may object to the doctor or attorney who has been designated, which objection is to be decided by the Justice presiding as a member of the panel (subd. 2, par. (d)). The panel hearings are informal and without stenographic records (subd. 4). As initially enacted section 148-a provided that no statement or expression of opinion made in the course of the hearing would be admissible in evidence either as an admission or otherwise in any trial of the action (subd. 4) and contained no provision for introduction of the panel's recommendation at any subsequent trial.

Subdivision 8, which was added by amendment in 1975 (L.1975, ch. 109 sec. 16), provides:

> If the three members of the panel concur as to the question of liability, a formal written recommendation concerning such question of liability shall be signed by the panel members and forwarded to all parties. In such event, the recommendation shall be admissible in evidence at any subsequent trial upon the request of any party to the action. The recommendation shall not be binding upon the jury or, in the case tried without a jury, upon the trial court, but shall be accorded such weight as the jury or the trial court chooses to ascribe to it.
>
> If the recommendation is read to the jury or by the trial court, the doctor member or the attorney member of the panel, or both of them, may be called as a witness by any party with reference to the recommendation of the panel only. The party calling such witness or witnesses shall pay their reasonable fees and expenses.

III. 1980 AD HOC COMMITTEE REPORT

The negative sentiments echoed by the lawyers involved in medical malpractice litigation apparently have been confirmed by the 1980 report of an ad hoc committee headed by Justice Joseph Gagliardi, Administrative Judge of the Ninth Judicial District, at the request of the Chief Administrative Judge of the State of New York. As a result of a statewide survey conducted by the committee to determine the connection between findings of medical malpractice panels and subsequent disposition of cases, the committee found: (1) that there is no greater propensity for the parties to settle during panel hearings; (2) that there is a general increase in the monetary amount of settlements and jury verdict; and (3) that the rate of settlement does not show an improvement. (*See* Report of the Ad Hoc Committee on Medical Malpractice Panels to the Chief Administrative Judge of the State of New York on the Operation of Medical Malpractice Panels, dated March 19, 1980.)

IV. PROCEDURAL DELAYS

The procedure which must be followed in order to satisfy the statute, Judiciary Law sec. 148-a, involves various steps, which cause delay in the disposition of cases. The initial step is to determine which medical specialty or specialities will consider a particular claim. Pursuant to statute, specifically paragraph 3b of Judiciary Law sec. 148-a, *supra,* the state or local medical society, upon review of the submitted written material, will designate the appropriate medical specialty involved. This one initial step could unduly encumber the whole system resulting in inordinate delays. Fortunately, the rules promulgated by the various appellate divisions have given considerable flexibility to this requirement. What has been followed and adopted in actual practice is to have all the attorneys enter into a stipulation (oral or written), in which they agree to the medical specialty or specialties that will be required to hear the contentions. Indeed, the judges assigned to the various medical malpractice parts have been successful in extracting agreements from the attorneys without the necessity of referring the matter to the medical society (a cumbersome process). Once the specialty has been selected, delay is often encountered in obtaining a physician within that specialty whose available time to sit on the panel coincides with that of the court who must convene a hearing. In addition, the panel member is expected to have spent whatever time is required in a review of the written materials (often voluminous) submitted by all parties to the court within a prescribed time prior to the hearing. Moreover, the panel member, be he physician or attorney, is cognizant of the spectre of being subpoenaed as a witness at trial, if a unanimous recommendation is made following the panel hearing. *See* Judiciary Law sec. 148-a, par. 8, *supra*.

Once the panel has been convened, the hearing held and the determination rendered, the case will be set down for trial and will work its way up the calendar. During this period, the justice presiding will convene one or more conferences (colloquially referred to as post-panel conferences) for the purpose of attempting to settle the case. The overall results of these conferences in items of achieving settlements and/or discontinuances prior to actual jury selection, have been disappointing. In short, court dockets are burgeoning and efforts made by court administrators to reduce them have been impeded.

V. PECUNIARY CONSIDERATIONS

The present system (compulsory medical malpractice panels in cases in which physicians and hospitals are defendants) carries with it a high price tag. The plaintiffs are saddled with increased costs and disbursements incurred in the additional steps necessitated by the panel hearing. As a result of the delays attendant upon the compulsory panel procedures, plaintiffs are deprived of an expeditious determination of their claims with ultimate compensation for their injuries (oftentimes protracted and permanent), if their claims are found to be valid. The very nature of the injuries may have deprived the plaintiff of an opportunity to be gainfully employed and the subsequent medical care and treatment and custodial care which may be necessary often will result in a drain of the plaintiff's savings. Clearly, the plaintiff has the most to lose when the ultimate resolution of his lawsuit is bogged down in the judicial process.

The defendant also shares in the pecuniary burden occasioned by the present compulsory panel system. Each step of the procedure entails time, energy and effort expended by defense counsel for which fees are charged, and rightly so. The costs of defending medical malpractice claims are, therefore, increased and are paid, in most circumstances, by the insurance carrier, who in turn passes on the increase to the physician policyholder. Moreover, during the pendency of the action, insurance carriers must establish reserves to provide for the possibility of ultimate payment to a successful plaintiff. Without doubt, these factors have contributed to the actual doubling of medical malpractice premiums during the period that the present system has been in place. Indeed, the present carrier, Medical Liability Mutual Insurance Company, run by the State Medical Society, had requested from its insureds less than one year ago, a rate increase of well over 100 percent. (A substantially smaller percentage increase was actually charged.)

VI. JUDGE-MADE ATTEMPTS TO BYPASS PANEL HEARINGS

Given the fact that the standard avenues for change are slow-going, one judge sitting in the malpractice part in the busiest county within this state has taken the "bull by the horns," so to speak, in an attempt to bypass the inordinate delays occasioned by the compulsory panel process. Recognizing that the panel was not authorized nor empowered to decide disputed issues of fact (indeed that would be tantamount to an unconstitutional invasion of the jury's province) Judge Ira Gammerman (Supreme Court, New York County, Medical Malpractice Part) has zealously scrutinized the facts and claims of the parties (by way of probing and incisive questions directed to the attorneys for all parties in open court) and has had occasion to decide that certain cases not be referred to a panel hearing because of the existence of threshhold questions not properly the subject of panel determination. Motions were made by litigants unhappy with the trial court's determination. Four motions were consolidated because of the sameness of the issues involved and were decided in *Rosa v. Mohan Kulkarni Unibell Anesthesia*, 113 Misc. 2d 39, 448 N.Y.S.2d 400 (Supreme Court, New York County, 1982).

In *Rosa*, *supra*, the court noted that three of the applications were brought by defendants seeking a medical malpractice panel. In one motion, it was the plaintiff who requested that his case be set down for trial without being submitted to a panel. Judge Gammerman's decision contains an analytical and illuminating discourse on the purposes and intent of the sponsors of the legislation that gave rise to the panels and on the frustrations, demand and burdens imposed on an already over-burdened system as a result of the compulsory panels. He shares with us his first-hand observations of the failure of the concept of the medical malpractice panel in achieving its desired goal.

The court observes in its decision in the *Rosa* case that "the panel is presented with a set of facts and reaches a conclusion based on those facts, much as an expert does when he testifies to an opinion based on facts postulated in the form of a hypothetical question." *Id.* 448 N.Y.S.2d at 402. However, the panel does not deal in hypotheticals, but will base its determination on facts with which there is no basic disagreement, according to the trial judge. He points out that it could not have been the legislative intent when enacting section 148-a that panels would resolve issues of fact or would make determinations of credibility, for to do so "would obviously transcend the outer limits of constitutional tolerance." *Id.* at 403.

Judge Gammerman concluded in *Rosa*, *supra*, that he had discretion to rule that certain cases were not to be submitted to a panel and that in each of the cases in question, a clear question of fact was raised between the parties which precluded a panel decision. Thus, the respective cases were directed to proceed to trial without submission to medical malpractice panel hearings.

The trial court in *Rosa v. Mohan Kulkarni Unibell Anesthesia*, *supra*, appears to be the first to have taken the bold step in predetermining that questions of fact with respect to medical issues exist thereby rendering the submission of the case to a medical panel an obvious waste of time. (Indeed, the medical panel is often constrained to vote "No Findings" when it is confronted with a factual dispute as to the medical treatment or lack thereof. A vote of "No Findings" leaves the parties in a situation of *status quo ante.*)

VII. APPELLATE REVIEW OF THE *ROSA* CASE AND ITS PROGENY

The unsuccessful litigants took an appeal from the order of the trial court in *Rosa*, *supra*, and were successful in obtaining a reversal, but by a slim margin of 3-2. *Rosa v. Kulkarni*, 89 A.D.2d 529, 452 N.Y.S.2d 441 (1st Dep't, 1982). The majority members of the court found that there were, indeed, issues of medical malpractice (gleaned from the plaintiffs' complaint) which would be within the purview of a malpractice panel. The Appellate Division did not address the issue of whether or not the trial court had discretion in the first place (within the confines of section 148-a) to rule that disputed questions existed and then to bypass submission of those cases to a medical panel.

It was the dissenting opinion of Judge Silverman in *Rosa*, *supra* (concurred in by Judge Kupferman) which confronted that particular issue. According to the dissenters, nothing in the statute, Judiciary Law sec. 148-a, or rules, Rule 636.1 of the Rules of the Appellate Division, First Department, deprived the trial judge of discretion to determine which cases were to be set down and which were not to be set down for a panel hearing. They agreed, moreover, that in this case the trial judge did not abuse his discretion in determining that it was unlikely that any useful purpose would be served by ordering that this case be heard before a medical panel. This conclusion was reached by the dissenting justices despite their finding that the "damage issue" (i.e., what the plaintiff's damages were) "may indeed involve some medical expertise." *Id.* 452 N.Y.S.2d at 443.

The sharply divided appellate court in the *Rosa* appeal, *supra*, is indicative of the tenuous fibers holding together the medical malpractice panel procedures. Perhaps it is even more indicative of the dissatisfaction held by prominent members of the judiciary with the effectiveness and usefulness of the system.

In *Gold v. Hershey*, 90 A.D.2d 704, 445 N.Y.S.2d 371 (1st Dep't, 1982), a case which followed the *Rosa* appeal by only four months, the Appellate Division once again had occasion to review an order of Judge Gammerman which denied defendants' motion for a hearing before a medical malpractice panel. As in *Rosa*, *supra*, the Court reversed the trial court's order (Judge Silverman concurred on constraint of *Rosa*) but again refused to consider "the permissible extent of the court's discretion under these circumstances." *Id.* at 372. Instead, the Court's decision was based on its holding that issues of medical malpractice existed which are within the province of a malpractice panel.

Several months following the *Gold* decision, *supra*, the Appellate Division in *Bleich v. Bono*, 91 A.D.2d 911, 457 N.Y.S.2d 795 (1st Dep't, 1983), again reversed an order of Judge Gammerman, which directed that certain medical malpractice cases not be submitted to panel. Again, as in *Gold* and *Rosa*, *supra*, the Court held that medical issues existed which warranted panel review.

However, in *Bleich*, the Court went a step further. Citing *Bernstein v. Bodean*, 53 N.Y.2d 520, 528, 443 N.Y.S.2d 49, 426 N.E.2d 741 (1981), the Court opined that the existence of disputed factual issues does not preclude reference to a panel. (Judge Silverman concurred, again on constraint of *Rosa v. Kulkarni*, *supra*.)

VIII. INROADS—LIMITING THE EFFECT OF A PANEL

The First Department's reliance on the *Bernstein* case (for the proposition that disputed factual issues do not preclude reference to a panel) is somewhat misleading. In *Bernstein v. Bodean*, *supra*, the Court of Appeals broadened the permissible scope of the cross-examination at trial of a physician member of the medical malpractice panel. That case suggests that the panelist may be examined concerning: (1) the recommendation itself; (2) panel procedures; (3) the data considered; (4) the opportunities for and extent of deliberation; (5) interim and final votes or statements of position by each panel member; (6) the professional and practical background of the panel recommendation; and (7) the factual and medical bases for and the processes by which the panel, individually and collectively, arrived at tentative and final conclusions.

The *Bernstein* Court looked to the language of the legislature (specifically the addition of subdivision 8 to section 148-a of the Judiciary Law) which allowed the panel's recommendation to be admissible at the trial and made available as witnesses the panel physician and attorney. In its decision, the Court made clear that "the objective of the statutory amendment allowing the introduction into evidence of the panel recommendation could only have been to assist the triers of fact in reaching a verdict. The role of the panel was not to supplant the jury (or the trial court, as the case might be); its recommendation was not intended to replace the jury's verdict (or that of the trial court)." *Id.* at 527.

Quite clearly, the Court of Appeals in *Bernstein v. Bodean*, *supra*, reinforced and strengthened the function of the jury (or the trial judge, if that be the case) in medical malpractice cases to decide all disputed issues, medical and nonmedical alike. The Court's purpose in that case was to allow scrutiny (by way of cross-examination) of the panelist's recommendation. Perhaps one may interpret this decision as being another inroad, however small, in the undoing of the panel process. Certainly, it bespeaks an increasing judicial concern for the operational effect of malpractice panels. One may not reasonably infer from the *Bernstein* case, however, that the Court of Appeals has condoned the submission to a medical panel of disputed factual issues.

IX. MORE INROADS—INSTRUCTIONS TO THE JURY—JUDGE'S CHARGE

Effective September of 1982, two amendments were made to the New York Pattern Jury Instructions (NY PJI) with respect to the receipt in evidence (during a jury trial) of the recommendation of the medical malpractice panel. Said amendments are numbered PJI 2:151A and PJI 2:151A.1, respectively.

The charge numbered PJI 2:151A is to be given to the jury at the point during the trial when the panel finding is first received in evidence. The trial court will charge the jury as follows:

> There has just been received in evidence the recommendation as to liability made by a panel appointed as provided by law. The panel consisted of a Justice of the Supreme Court, a doctor and a lawyer. Before making its recommendation, the panel held an informal hearing with the attorneys present and also reviewed hospital and medical records.

> The recommendation is not controlling on your judgment, but is presented to assist you in reaching a proper verdict in this case. You may accept or reject it, depending upon whether you agree or disagree with it after consideration of all the evidence in the case.

Thereafter, at the conclusion of the testimony and during the trial judge's main charge to the jury, the following will be given to the jury (PJI 2:151A.1):

> During the trial there was received in evidence a recommendation as to liability by a panel consisting of a judge, a doctor and a lawyer. I told you then, and now I remind you, that the recommendation is not binding upon you but is to be considered by you along with all the other evidence in the case.
>
> You also heard the testimony of (Dr. AB, Mr. CD) (a) member(s) of the panel. (His, their) testimony is also not binding upon you, but is to be considered along with all the other evidence in the case.

(The second paragraph of this charge will be given only if one of the panel members is called as a witness by any one of the parties.)

The amendments reflect a change from prior practice which provided for only one charge concerning the panel to be given at the conclusion of the trial, i.e., during the court's main charge to the jury. Apparently, the purpose of giving the jury the additional instruction (PJI 2:151A) (at the point during the trial when the panel findings are received and made known to the jury) is to reinforce in the minds of the jurors the concept that they are the sole and final judges of the facts of the case. Moreover, the apparent intent of the amendments is to ameliorate the effect of the panel recommendation so as to further ensure that it not supplant or constrain the freedom of the jury's consideration. *See* Comment to PJI 2:151A, 1 NY PJI 2d 168 (supp.).

X. CONSTITUTIONALITY—OTHER STATES

Screening panel procedures which had been established in two other states have been declared invalid by the highest court of each state upon the ground that, although facially valid, the practical effect of the implementation of the screening procedures violated procedural due process and the right to a jury trial. *See Aldana v. Holub*, 381 So.2d 231 (Fla., 1980); *Mattos v. Thompson*,

491 Pa. 385, 421 A.2d 190 (1980). Although both state statutes were substantially different from the New York procedure, both cases are illustrative of the initiative taken by some courts to defeat medical malpractice screening procedures.

XI. CONSTITUTIONALITY—NEW YORK STATE

Interestingly enough, in this state, the issue of the constitutionality of the legislation establishing medical malpractice panels has not been directly confronted by our highest Court. The case which is generally accepted to be that upon which the statute had passed constitutional muster is *Comiskey v. Arlen*, 55 A.D.2d 304, 390 N.Y.S.2d 122 (2nd Dep't, 1976), *aff'd on other grounds*, 43 N.Y.2d 696, 401 N.Y.S.2d 200 (1977). However, although the Appellate Division in that case unanimously held the statute constitutional on the theory that the introduction of a unanimous panel finding is, in effect, an expert opinion which is to be evaluated by the jury in the same manner as it would evaluate any other expert opinion, the Court of Appeals affirmed *Comiskey, without reaching the constitutional issue*, on the ground that it would be premature to make the decision (of constitutionality) until the issue was raised after trial and judgment. *See also Bernstein v. Bodean*, *supra*.

Comiskey v. Arlen, *supra*, was decided prior to the issuance of the Ad Hoc Committee Report, *supra,* and without the benefit of the findings made by that Committee. Perhaps in view of the conclusions of said Committee, the constitutionality of section 148-a should be, once and for all, carefully evaluated.

XII. PROPOSAL FOR CHANGE

In view of the widespread dissatisfaction with the present system, legislation has been submitted, through the auspices of the Unified Court System, that would replace the present system of mandatory medical malpractice panels with a method of rigorous calendar control and case management and an optional medical malpractice mediation panel. Under the proposed system, a panel (composed of the same members who now sit) would convene only at the parties' request and would mediate and crystalize the issues and press for settlement of the action in appropriate cases. Moreover, unlike the present system, the panel's recommendation would not be admissible at a subsequent trial. *See* Cooke, *Medical Malpractice Panels—Cooke Sees Failure in System*, Vol. 189 No. 48, NYLJ, p. 1, col. 2, 3/11/83.

XIII. CONCLUSION

The time has come, if not overdue, for legislative action substantially revamping, modifying or, better still, repealing the entire section of the law which compels medical malpractice panel hearings. While awaiting legislative mandate, the courts, we have seen, have grappled with the myriad procedural problems encountered as a result of the panel process and have taken the initiative—have made inroads—into lessening or ameliorating the impact of the panel recommendation on the jury process and into unclogging the calendar congestion occasioned by the cumbersome procedure.

Much has been done towards reforming the present system of compulsory medical malpractice panels; much more remains to be done. To prevent total collapse in the mediation and resolution of medical malpractice claims, delay in its reformation should not be countenanced.

CHAPTER EIGHT

THE DEPOSITION OF THE DEFENDANT PHYSICIAN

Richard E. Shandell, Esq.

This article is based on material from *The Preparation and Trial of Medical Malpractice Cases* by Richard Shandell, published and copyrighted by Law Journal Seminars-Press, 111 Eighth Avenue, New York, NY 10011.

I. THE DEPOSITION OF THE DEFENDANT PHYSICIAN

It is almost axiomatic in a medical malpractice case that the defendants have control of the facts. It follows from that basic axiom that the case will have to be tried along lines that assume that the events are as the defendant described them. Taking the events as the defendant describes them, you must prove that his treatment failed to meet minimally acceptable standards of practice. Sometimes, because of naivete, arrogance or poor preparation, or a combination of these factors, the defendant, at the deposition, will have so incriminated himself that there is no defense left available. More frequently, no such happy circumstance will occur. At a minimum, however, you wish to build fences through which he cannot escape so that at the trial his defenses can be broken down.

As you face the deposition, you should be in the following position: There has been a self-evidently serious injury or death owing to the failure of the treatment to yield the hoped for results; or an unexpected complication that has arisen. The medical literature indicates that a proper form of treatment, not employed in this case, could have yielded better results, or avoided the complication. Your expert has concluded, from his study of the records of the case, that the defendant's failure to employ such a course constituted malpractice, and that the malpractice was a cause of the bad result.

II. POSSIBLE DEFENSES

At the deposition, the defendant has available to him a number of possible defenses.

A. The defendant may set up defenses outside the scope of the standard. One device frequently employed for evading the standard you seek to impose is to blame the patient for the bad result, claiming that:

1. The patient was too fat (obese);

2. The patient has unusual anatomy (severely scarred inside from previous surgery, for instance);

3. The patient did not follow instructions;

4. The patient did not return to the doctor's office, where proper treatment would have been administered on the next visit;

5. The patient never informed the physician of a significant element in the patient's history;

6. The patient refused the treatment recommended;

7. The patient suffered from additional ailments not recorded or not recognized at the time, which made his actual condition worse than it seemed.

B. Another important means of avoiding the application of the standard is to describe the actual treatment as different from that which is recorded. For example, the defendant may say that tests and examinations were performed but not recorded, because their results were "negative" or "normal."

He can admit the material facts but contest their medical significance. He may, for example, take the position that the test which you say he should have performed was too dangerous and, therefore, contraindicated.

C. He may contest causal connection. The problems in this aspect of the case are so bothersome and so endemic to a medical malpractice lawsuit that the issue merits separate discussion. It suffices to say, at present, that disputing causal connection and blaming the patient constitute the two most prevalent defenses to a medical malpractice case. It is comparatively rare that a case will be tried as a simple contest of opinion in which the two parties cannot agree on the proper standards of accepted practice.

1. A dispute on the issue of causal connection usually takes one of two forms. In the first, the defendant asserts that the plaintiff's injuries arose from a course of events different from the explanation for the injuries at which you and your expert have arrived. This claimed source of the plaintiff's injury may be a virus or other infection, a heart attack, a coughing spell, etc. A defense of this sort may be combined, for best results, with blaming the patient. The patient coughed, or fell, or was too fat, or was an alcoholic, or did not give a proper history, etc.

2. The other common form of a contest on the issue of causal connection is for the defense to take the position that either the patient or the patient's

leg, or kidney, uterus, etc., was doomed and that there was, therefore, no point in torturing him/her with all those tests or treatments because his/her condition was irredeemably hopeless.

D. A proper deposition will eliminate as many defenses as possible and fence in any that remain, so that the defendant and his expert cannot escape effective cross-examination at the trial. At a minimum, the following must be established at a deposition of the defendant:

1. Defendant's education, training, qualifications and hospital affiliations.

2. The extent of defendant's recollection of the patient and the course of treatment, without reference to the records. All details should be recalled. Remember, one must be aware of the need to foreclose, to the extent possible, eleventh-hour testimony about events and circumstances not in the records. The temptation for the defendant to testify to tests, examinations and other alleged circumstances not heretofore disclosed so as to meet your expert's criticisms is great. You must see to it that he unburdens himself fully at the deposition; all potential surprises must come to light here.

3. The occasion when the defendant first saw the patient.

4. The medical history which the defendant received, including the questions the physician asked to secure this history and the medical significance that the physician attached to the history. When the defendant attempts to avoid liability by blaming the patient's prior operations, obesity, unusual sensitivity, etc., remember that this defendant had never asked about or attached medical significance to these points when he originally took the history.

5. The examination the defendant performed in detail—not merely a statement of the findings. Eventually, the doctor is going to say that his examination included things he did not record because the results of these unrecorded tests were normal. Get the complete examination down in detail. For example, if he says he did a neurological examination, get the details. A complete neurological examination takes thirty minutes. Unless he is a neurologist, the defendant's so-called neurological examination was probably completed in thirty seconds.

6. The tests the defendant performed, the results and the medical significance thereof.

7. The defendant's findings and the medical significance of each finding.

8. The differential diagnosis and the basis of the diagnosis. In doing a differential diagnosis, a physician will list all the possible diagnoses, more or less, in order of probability.

9. The defendant's advice to the plaintiff, including all conversation. This will preclude the doctor from later saying that the patient disobeyed instructions or did not come back or was a chronic complainer, etc.

10. The treatment, the reason for each aspect of treatment and what the doctor hoped to accomplish thereby.

11. The defendant's opinion as to any available communications from other doctors, in the form of letters, reports or hospital communications, such as progress notes, consultation reports, or X-ray reports, and the medical significance the defendant attached to the findings and conclusions of other doctors.

12. The surgery, if performed, in detail. The surgeon must relate every aspect of the operation, minute by minute, tissue by tissue, structure by structure. Do not allow the surgeon merely to read the operative report.

Repeat all of the above steps for each contact between the physician and the patient in the office, home or hospital. Be sure, also, to secure a copy of the physician's records. Mark them for identification.

If you have gone through the above, you have created the parameters within which the case will be tried. Your control over the case depends on your control over those parameters. Although the defendant has control over the facts, the medical records and the depositions should create the fences with which you can achieve control over the issues to be tried. The object is to prevent the defendant, during the trial, from jumping over the fences and creating new defenses for which you are not prepared. Now that you have built the fences, the time has come to smoke out the defense. If the defendant had jumped outside the medical records during his deposition, it may be that the trial will boil down to the question whether the plaintiff's version, based on the medical records, is the correct rendition of events or whether the defendant's version, unbolstered by written materials, is the more accurate. This position is not an easy position for the defendant. It may be that a sufficiently bright, articulate and personable physician can convince the jury that the records are in error, but he will do so with some difficulty.

If, on the other hand, the defendant has admitted to the facts as contained in the medical records, and agreed with your version of events, you are down to a dispute over the accepted form of treatment, which is, as I have said, comparatively rare.

There may, of course, also be a defense based upon the absence of causal connection between the alleged negligent acts or omissions and the end result.

III. RECENT CASES

The legal tools necessary to smoke out the defense are contained in a series of recent cases. Several courts have held that at the trial the plaintiff may call defendant to the stand and elicit opinion evidence. The same privilege has since been extended to the plaintiff's examinations of the defendant before trial, both as to the latter's factual knowledge and his expert opinion, "for the purpose of establishing the generally accepted medical practice in the community." By way of dictum, one court stated that the privilege did not extend to examining the witness about the quality of treatment of a codefendant. The Court, however, allowed the plaintiff to examine the defendant, a vascular surgeon called in to treat circulatory problems in the patient's leg, about postoperative care in handling an appendectomy. Another court, however, allowed the plaintiff to depose a nonparty employee of the defendant hospital as to his medical opinion regarding the cause of decedent's death, even though such opinion also related to services provided by defendant doctor.

In another case, the plaintiff was permitted to examine a nonparty witness to ascertain the practice in administering pitocin. Here, the witness had originally been named as a defendant but had never been served. The court allowed the testimony, even though the witness denied knowledge of the administration of the drug. Finally, a pediatrician was required to answer questions as to his knowledge of the effect on a baby of medicines given by the codefendant obstetrician.

IV. THE "WHY" QUESTION

Malpractice is an intellectual tort. The most important question one can ask at a deposition of a defendant doctor is **why**.

Doctor, what was your diagnosis? **Why?**
What other diagnoses did you consider? **Why?**
Did you reject these others? **Why?**
What treatment did you employ? **Why?**
Did you consider other treatment? **Why?**
Did you reject other treatment? **Why?**

If you get objections to **why** questions, these objections have no basis whatsoever, but sometimes defense lawyers have confused the tactical rule that you should not, at trial, ask **why** questions with some rule of law that prohibits them. If some defendant makes such objections, you can always substitute "What was the reason?" or "What was the purpose?" or "What was the basis for your decision?" for **why**.

V. CONCLUSION

A. Finally, the defendant must be asked the following:

1. Do you have an opinion, doctor, as to the cause of the patient's (death, loss of kidney, etc.)? If yes, what is your opinion? What is the basis for your opinion?

2. Do you know of any precaution that could have prevented the patient's (death, loss of kidney, etc.)?

3. In your opinion, was it a departure from accepted practice to have (omitted an angiogram)? What is the basis for your opinion?

You do not really care what the answers are. You are building the fences that will prevent the defendant's escape later on. What you want is to eliminate as many defenses as possible, narrowing the issues so that you can mount overwhelming evidence against the remaining defense. Keep in mind that while you are narrowing the issues, the defense attorney will attempt to increase the number of issues and multiply and combine defenses. You will try to persuade the jury to see only one issue, namely whether your view of the case, based on the medical records, or the defendant's version, represents the correct rendition of events. The defense attorney will try to obfuscate the nature of the claims so that the jury will see many issues.

B. Lastly, a claim of a lack of informed consent often elicits the defense that the injury was one of the risks of the procedure. It is important to inquire whether there was any discussion of the risks of the procedure and if so, what was said. If the injury truly was one of the risks, you want to know why there was no warning of it. Normally, if the physician testified that he warned specifically of the risks of the very injury suffered, the jury will not believe him. If he fails to include such a warning, this omission may cast some doubt on the credibility of his claim that the plaintiff's injury is a risk of the procedure. Informed consent, as a theory of recovery, has a very limited applicability. However, it may assume great tactical importance at the trial.

CHAPTER NINE

THE DEPOSITION OF THE PLAINTIFF

Peter C. Kopff, Esq.

I. GOALS

The pretrial deposition of a claimant provides the attorney for the defendant with an opportunity to learn about the plaintiff and his claims. There is a duty to the defendant client to conduct the deposition in a manner which will confine the plaintiff and wherever possible prevent or minimize the risk of surprises at trial. Goals include:

1. Identify injuries.
2. Obtain claimant's recollection of the underlying events.
3. Obtain favorable admissions.
4. Obtain testimony which can be used to undermine claimant's credibility at trial.

Evaluate the claimant's "jury appeal." Appearance, personality, demeanor, recollection and temperament all influence your impression of the patient's honesty.

II. TECHNIQUE

Technique of questioning is variable. Allow the witness to talk at length. Preserve your objections where the answer goes beyond the scope of the questions and where the testimony is damaging.

Tie the witness down on crucial areas: Do you recall any other presurgical conversations with Dr. Scapel? Did you make any other complaints to Dr. Housecall?

You must listen to the witness so you can properly follow up on information. If you question a witness from a rigid list of questions, you will lose the opportunity to gain valuable information by following up on the claimant's response. A checklist is useful solely as a general guide for major areas you do not wish to omit.

III. PREPARATION

A. Review pertinent medical and hospital records. Notations of initial history, physical examinations and nursing notes provide valuable details concerning the patient's condition, complaints, symptoms or lack thereof. I prefer to prepare a handwritten "chronology" outlining salient features prior to the claimant's deposition. Questioning the plaintiff on specific points which are documented in medical records can be particularly useful at trial if the claimant's credibility proves to be "unreliable." A jury will frequently accept a nurse's notation over a claimant's recollection. The pretrial deposition should properly be used to lay the foundation for inconsistencies.

B. Review the pleadings. If there is no claim for lack of informed consent or lost earnings, your questioning can accordingly be modified. Where boilerplate injuries are incorporated, ask specifically about dubious items and you will frequently obtain favorable admissions.

C. Review pertinent medical literature. The defense attorney's own study of medical textbooks or journals can be an objective source of information and may suggest a useful line of questions.

D. Determine the patient's primary language so an interpreter can be arranged if necessary.

E. Documents such as loan applications, employment records, school records, mortgage applications, leasehold applications and applications for life insurance can be valuable sources of statements which a plaintiff may readily contradict at his deposition. Many of these documents can be obtained prior to pretrial depositions with a little initiative and investigative savy. These documents should not be used to confront the claimant directly at the pretrial stage. They are used to direct questions so that a foundation for impeachment of the witness is available at trial.

IV. CONDUCTING THE DEPOSITION

A. Introduction

Introduce yourself. Tell the witness whom you represent. Remind him to answer only if he understands the question. You will gladly rephrase the question if it is confusing.

1. Determine medications the patient has taken today:

a. dosage
b. pharmacy
c. prescribing physician

2. Languages: Determine the patient's primary language and what languages he uses at home and with treating physicians. Establish that he understands English. He was able to read English such as in the "surgical consent," "discharge instruction to patient" and "refusal of treatment" forms he signed.

3. Documents he reviewed in preparation for his testimony including:

a. diary
b. notes
c. medical records
d. literature
e. medication containers or prescription forms—identify and obtain copies (if the witness' recollection is based upon or corroborated by a diary or notations, find out now, not during the trial)
f. photographs, movies
g. any other documentary evidence

B. Topics

1. Present Complaints. Try to confine the witness. If he complains of pain, inquire as to what physician he last made these complaints; what analgesics he has taken, when and how frequently:

a. duration
b. severity
c. medications

If there is a claim of emotional or psychological injury, inquire about visits with psychiatrists, psychologists, clergymen or counselors.

From your prior review of the relevant medical records you have noted nurse and physician's notes of "no complaints" at certain dates and times. Ask specifically if the patient had complaints at those dates and times. The witness' credibility or the reliability and his testimony must be tested.

2. Present activities (Use your imagination)

a. work
b. home
c. recreation
d. household chores
e. marital status
f. date of birth
g. social activities

3. Residence

a. house or apartment
b. duration of residency
c. residency last ten years
d. location of bedroom (floor)
e. addresses
f. vacation home

4. Education—Any family member in a medical field?

5. Employment

a. duties
b. duration
c. income
d. medical insurance (in New York State substantive law allows reduction of medical malpractice verdict by third party payments)

6. Other names by which plaintiff is or was known.

7. Identify other witness: Did a family member accompany the claimant? Who else was present when Dr. Scapel discussed the contemplated surgery?

8. Treating Physicians

a. name
b. office address
c. specialty
d. when seen

e. where seen
f. why seen
g. patient's complaints
h. medical history given to this physician
i. other witnesses present
j. examination performed
k. treatment
l. medications (prescription or samples)
m. diagnostic tests
n. bill

9. Hospitalizations

a. name and location
b. when treated

(1) each admission
(2) out-patient and clinic care

c. nature of treatment
d. private physician's patient or hospital service clinic patient
e. complaints
f. history given
g. with whom patient spoke
h. who examined
i. diagnostic tests and devices (X-ray, scans)
j. anesthesia
k. medications
l. identify other patients in room or other witnesses
m. bills

10. Complaints and Symptoms

a. chronologically
b. what complaints, nature, frequency, character
c. duration
d. severity
e. to whom made (nurses, physicians)
f. medications (analgesics)

g. procedures, exercises, rehabilitation
h. patient's own records if any
i. activities, recreation

11. Damages

a. lost earnings
b. medical expenses

(1) medications
(2) physician
(3) hospital
(4) nursing

12. Occupation

a. present and past employment
b. duties, nature of work, title
c. salary
d. hours
e. physical exam required
f. union membership
g. training
h. medical background or training if any
i. dates missed from work because of illness
j. medical insurance

13. Education

a. final grade completed
b. schools attended
c. school missed because of disabilities
d. military service

14. Informed Consent

a. Before seeing Dr. Scapel, what had other physicians told you?

b. Before seeing Dr. Scapel, what had you read or learned from friends or other patients?

c. What did Dr. Scapel tell you about the surgery?

(1) risks
(2) alternative treatment
(3) prognosis with and without surgery

15. Family Medical History

a. Any history of relevant disease(s) in patient's siblings, parents or grandparents.

b. Cause of death of parents and grandparents.

V. CONCLUDING THE DEPOSITION

Keep in mind your goal of confining the plaintiff's claims. To avoid the unpleasant surprise of new claims at trial, finish up areas of inquiry with questions that will tie down the witness.

A. Did you have any other conversations with Dr. Scapel at any time?

B. Do you recall any other conversations with any personnel of Mercy Hospital prior to your discharge?

VI. REPORT

Your impression of the jury appeal of the witness should be recorded for other lawyers who will evaluate the case. The transcript of testimony will not reflect appearance, demeanor and other qualities that a jury will consider in deciding credibility.

Your client also deserves your evaluation of the impact of the witness' testimony on the defensibility of the case and on the judgment and settlement value of the case.

VII. FOLLOW-UP

Obtain hospital, physicians, medical, pharmacy and employment records which you have learned of during this deposition. Take necessary steps to obtain the pretrial testimony of witnesses of whom you have learned.

Obtain information and documents promised by the witness and counsel during E.B.T.

CHAPTER TEN

CHECKLIST FOR DEPOSITION OF THE PLAINTIFF AND DEFENDANT FROM DEFENDANT'S VIEWPOINT

Joseph M. Costello, Esq.

I. PREPARATION FOR DEPOSITION OF PLAINTIFF

A. Analysis of Pleadings

1. Bill of Particulars—important to know specific claims of malpractice, lack of informed consent, damages, treating physicians and medical institutions

2. Interrogatories responded to in Federal Court

B. Notice to Take E.B.T.—serve contemporaneously with Answer and Demand for Bill of Particulars (Interrogatories in Federal Court)

1. Priority of testimony—plaintiff will go first, then the defendant

2. Include in Notice the production of medical bills, prescriptions, appointment books, cards, etc.

C. Medical Records Reviewed

1. Sent for and received key medical records, at least the hospital records of incident in question, and physician's records; this is assuming you have demanded and received authorizations from plaintiff's counsel

2. In-house review of records

D. Plaintiff's Background and Claim Reviewed

1. Possible investigation of plaintiff's background

2. Review in detail with your client his relationship with the plaintiff from personal and professional standpoint

E. Medical Literature Review—Generally

F. Make Outline of General Areas of Questioning

G. Hire Court Reporter That Has Done Malpractice Cases

II. DEPOSITION OF PLAINTIFF

A. Family Background—Generally

B. Medical History—Depending on Claim of Malpractice

1. Family medical history—hereditary inherited diseases, syndromes or malformations in children, brother and sisters or other family members

a. brain-damaged children
b. cancer cases

2. Plaintiff's medical background in detail prior to contact with your physician

C. All Contacts Had and Conversation With Your M.D. On All Occasions and Other Party Defendants

1. Specifics of office visits

2. All medications prescribed

3. Details of conversations with doctor and his/her staff

D. All Contacts and Details of Any and All Treating Physicians and Hospital's

E. Details of Claims of Special Damages

1. Production of medical bills

2. Interrogate as to specific problems or limitations experienced

3. Prosthetic or therapeutic devices

III. PREPARATION FOR DEPOSITION OF YOUR CLIENT PHYSICIAN

A. Review All Medical Records

B. Meet Your Physician At Least Twice Before E.B.T. (Examination Before Trial)

1. Initial conference

a. review medical records and his notes in detail

b. review pleadings gencrally

2. Meeting prior to E.B.T.

a. review plaintiff's testimony with doctor

b. review all records where he made notes in detail

c. make your client feel at ease—explain how the E.B.T. will be conducted, i.e., court reporter, parties present

C. Try To Schedule E.B.T. at Your Office—M.D. Will Feel More Comfortable

D. Photocopy Extra Copies of M.D.'s Records For All Parties—Make Sure M.D. Brings Originals to E.B.T.

E. M.D.'s Records—only produce office records of patient, not material prepared for litigation or correspondence between the M.D. and lawyer and M.D. and insurance carrier

F. Advise Doctor to Pause Before Answering

1. Provides doctor with time to think about answer

2. Provides the attorney with time to object to the question

IV. ATTENDANCE AT E.B.T. WITH M.D. CLIENT DEFENDANT

A. Produce Records For All Counsel—will make E.B.T. go quicker and smoother

B. Try to Limit Testimony to Client's Care and Treatment of Patient

C. Keep M.D.'s Answers Short and to the Question—don't allow extensive explanations unless you know the answer

D. Object to Questions As to Form—don't allow M.D. to answer; practically, by the time the question is in proper form, your M.D. will have time to think about his answer

E. Rulings on Objected Nonanswered Questions

1. Preferred practice—obtain rulings by written motion to the Court

2. If in Courthouse and you have to go for rulings, wait until the end of all questions and then go

CHAPTER ELEVEN

CHECKLIST FOR OBTAINING AN EXPERT WITNESS FOR THE DEFENDANT

Luke M. Pittoni, Esq.

I. WHEN SHOULD YOU OBTAIN THE EXPERT?

A. Before E.B.T.'s
B. Prior to Medical Malpractice Panel
C. Prior to trial

II. WHERE DO YOU OBTAIN AN EXPERT?

A. Consult the defendant
B. Subsequent treating doctors
C. Review literature—authors on subject
D. Directory of Medical Specialties
E. Medical Directory of NYS (Hospital Section)
F. Consult private investigator on case

III. HOW DO YOU OBTAIN AN EXPERT?

A. Visit the expert (be prepared)
B. If covering letter by attorney, this is discoverable
C. Stress need for honest opinion
D. *Note*: Guide the expert with attorney's analyses and theories

IV. SHOULD THE EXPERT FURNISH A WRITTEN REPORT?

A. Most cases avoid report
B. Consult with expert before any written report
C. Report is discoverable at trial
D. Report can be useful for Panel

V. WHAT MATERIAL SHOULD BE SENT TO EXPERT?

A. *All* medical records
B. *All* E.B.T. testimony
C. At trial: trial testimony of plaintiff's expert

VI. HOW MANY EXPERTS?

A. Within the same specialty of defendant
B. Outside specialty of defendant

1. Relating to liability
2. Relating to damages

C. At trial

1. Use as few as possible
2. Multiple specialties to prove defendant aspects of case

D. Can have others for advice, panel, etc.

VII. WHAT SPECIALTY OR SUBSPECIALTY SHOULD BE CONSULTED?

VIII. WHAT TO AVOID IN SELECTING AN EXPERT

A. Avoid overused experts
B. Avoid the "hired gun" expert

IX. THE ROLE OF THE EXPERT IN PREPARATION STAGES

A. To determine whether the case is defensible
B. To assist in preparing the defendant for his deposition
C. To assist in preparation for Medical Malpractice Panel
D. To guide the attorney as to the best defense

CHAPTER TWELVE

OBTAINING, PREPARING AND USING AN EXPERT WITNESS FOR THE PLAINTIFF

Steven E. Pegalis, Esq.
and
Harvey F. Wachsman, M.D., J.D.

I. INTRODUCTION

Since a medical malpractice trial often becomes a "battle of the experts," the subject of this article is of course critical for plaintiff's counsel. We do not intend to set forth a list of expert witnesses in this article. Suffice it to say that medical-legal experts may be available depending upon the case, and just who is involved. By and large, it is our feeling that obtaining a medical-legal expert is impossible on the impossible case. It is always difficult to obtain the proper medical-legal expert, and we have found that the degree of difficulty often correlates with the specialties involved.

Medical-legal experts may be obtained on occasion by approaching subsequent treating doctors; through recommendations from friends or medical colleagues; references from other attorneys, and/or determining experts who have testified for the plaintiff in other cases; and by approaching physicians in various specialties, who are known to have certain knowledge and expertise. One may analogize the acquiring of the appropriate medical-legal expert as a courtship process requiring a careful and intelligent approach and handling. The idea is to establish a professional relationship between attorney and medical-legal expert, which may be utilized to the mutual benefit of both. This is a relationship that once acquired must thereafter be carefully nurtured. Only in this way can plaintiff's counsel appropriately represent the interests of his client.

We have not had experience with the medical-legal service agencies that are often advertised. These service agencies represent that they will acquire specialists for review and testimony. We really cannot recommend for or against the use of such agencies. We do, however, have some concern about a "collateral" attack on a physician, who has been acquired through such an agency. Defense counsel will suggest that the expert witness voluntarily placed his name with this agency, so that he may acquire his fee. They will further suggest that the expert is more interested in his fee than the truth. A suggestion will be made that the expert witness is nothing more than a "hired gun," whose testimony has been bought by the plaintiff. Certainly, it is preferable for the plaintiff to present an expert in the context of being a concerned and honest physician who is reluctantly rendering an honest opinion on the quality of medical care. In this setting, compensation for the expert's valuable time may be viewed as a routine irrelevancy.

Retired physicians may be another fertile source for obtaining medical-legal experts. The retired physician, however, will be challenged as to whether or not he has kept abreast, and further, may be collaterally attacked on the contention that having now left active practice, the physician is merely supplementing a retirement income without concern for what is, or is not, the truth. In the right setting, and with the right preparation, however, a retired physician who has the requisite qualifications may well be a formidable and valuable expert for the plaintiff.

II. APPROACHING THE PROSPECTIVE MEDICAL-LEGAL EXPERT

Assuming plaintiff's counsel has from some source the name of a prospective medical-legal expert, the initial approach and presentation is quite important. Carelessly handled, plaintiff's counsel may lose a prospective expert, who may otherwise have been invaluable.

If possible, the expert should be approached at a time in which he is not harried or distracted. The expert should be told up front the circumstance by which you come to him, and if possible, you should request an opportunity to meet with the expert and discuss the matter. The expert should be advised that on behalf of your client, you seek his advice in order to better enable you to represent your client. You should tactfully explain that you are aware that this expert's time is limited and valuable, and that it is routine to compensate said expert for the imposition on his time. By "tactfully," we mean that the reference to payment not appear to be a bribe, but rather an obvious and ethical routine course of events.

It may be quite pointful to set forth who is or may be a defendant. In this way, the prospective expert may choose to decline, based on a prior relationship, or contact with a prospective defendant. Considerable judgment, however, must be used in this regard. We have had many circumstances in which an expert has given us constructive advice on a case, but yet, declined to testify, because of who the defendant is. We never view our relationship with an expert on a one-shot basis. Once the relationship exists, more often than not, it will prove to be beneficial and valuable in the future.

Before the initial contact, you certainly should know as much about your prospective expert as you possibly can. Obviously, if a prospetive expert is affiliated with the defendant hospital, it would be unwise to approach this physician in this particular case. The same expert may be valuable in a different case with a different defendant. One prominent expert, who we know, testified in a case, and was thereafter contacted by an attorney, who had heard the fact that he had so testified. This attorney, however, knew nothing of this expert's credentials. After introducing himself, and advising this expert of his desire for a medical-legal consultation, this attorney asked the expert: "Doctor, are you Board Certified?" This expert, who is a prominent professor and author, as well as the chairman of a major hospital department, politely terminated the conversation, and refused to deal with this attorney—feeling the attorney to be a fool, and interpreting the attorney's question to be in the nature of an insulting interview. This latter circumstance came to our attention, of course, from this prominent expert, with whom we have had a professional relationship for some years. We recall our initial contact with this expert some years ago, when he was involved as a subsequent treating doctor in a pending case. While not helpful on that particular case, we nevertheless were able to establish a polite and courteous dialogue, and suggested that it was unfortunate that patients involved in medical-legal disputes did not have more ready access to medical-legal experts of his caliber and experience. It was not so long thereafter that this expert agreed to review a case for us, and things flowed from there.

III. WHAT DO YOU GIVE THE MEDICAL-LEGAL EXPERT FOR REVIEW?

The initial response to this question at first blush may appear to be—"all the records." However, some discretion is in order. A huge pile of records may "turn off" a busy medical-legal expert. On the other hand, inadequate or insufficient records may achieve the same result. Hopefully, plaintiff's counsel will understand enough about his case, and have complete enough records to at least initially furnish the expert with a nonburdensome supply of records. It is also pointful to make certain that the photocopy of the records is "readable." Sometimes, the handwriting has been clarified with pretrial depositions. A little time spent "extracting" the depositions, thereby making it easier for the expert to read and review the material, may well reap dividends. Of course, ultimately, if the medical-legal expert is to testify at trial, it would be necessary for this physician to have and review every medical record which, if not read or reviewed, might form the basis of a cross-examination attack.

An often overlooked area of review are pertinent X-rays and/or pathology slides. Plaintiff's counsel frequently will assume that the X-rays and/or pathology slides accurately correspond with the written reports and hospital records. A sometimes effective maneuver employed by defense counsel is an attempt to make an unanticipated issue in this regard. For example, defense counsel may ask your expert:

Q: Doctor, did you review the X-ray films?

A: No, I did not.

Q: Are you basing your opinion on the assumption that the written report is accurate?

A: I am.

Q: So, therefore, you formulated your expert opinion in this case without ever looking at the X-rays?

A: That's correct.

Q: Did you ever ask to see the X-rays?

A: I did not.

Q: Doctor, before rendering an opinion in this case, may we assume that you did not feel it necessary to trouble yourself with the effort of reviewing these X-rays?

A: No one asked me to look at the X-rays.

If, as part of the defense, the X-rays are demonstratively placed up on a shadowbox, defense counsel may effectively create a diverting issue, and a ready-made collateral attack on your expert. Obviously, this is not a situation that will arise in every case. But from time to time, such a circumstance may importantly rear itself in a trial. Plaintiff's counsel should at least give this concept some forethought and consideration. Had there been appropriate preparation, this cross-examination may have gone as follows:

Q: Doctor, I noticed in your direct examination, you made no reference to reviewing the X-rays, isn't that correct?

A: That's true, I made no reference to reviewing the X-rays.

Q: Therefore, may we assume that you did not personally look at the X-rays, but rather, relied on the report in the chart?

A: No, you may not assume that. I did review the X-rays.

Q: You did? May we assume that you felt it not an important subject to mention on your direct testimony?

A: My interpretation of the X-rays was consistent with what was reported in the hospital record, and therefore, I felt there was no need to mention my personal review.

Obviously, the latter approach has taken the steam out of this "surprise" defense. Even if defense counsel introduces evidence suggesting an inaccuracy in the hospital X-ray report, the impact would be dramatically lessened. Plaintiff's expert, personally, corroborated the "official" hospital report, and there can be no defense argument that the plaintiff's expert was basing his opinion on an erroneous interpretation of the X-rays.

IV. HOW DOES ONE USE THE MEDICAL-LEGAL EXPERT?

Obviously, the use of the medical-legal expert will vary from case to case, and from attorney to attorney. The following are the possible uses of the medical-legal expert by plaintiff's counsel:

1. Initial evaluation of facts and circumstances presented by the client. Is this a case worth pursuing in the first place?

2. Initial review of hospital and medical records in order to determine whether there is or is not a valid case, and if so, who should be included as party defendants.

3. Specialty review of X-rays, pathology slides, sonogram, mammography, CAT scan, etc., may be appropriate in order to determine if there is a case, or how to proceed with a case.

4. Assisting counsel in locating and obtaining various medical literature that may be pointful in the case.

5. Assisting counsel in preparing for and taking depositions of defense witnesses.

6. Assisting counsel in determining what, if any, other discovery procedures are in order. For example, the expert may feel it necessary to learn what a subsequent treating doctor found, thereby, perhaps, requiring a deposition of a nonparty witness.

7. In certain circumstances, the expert may be deposed as part of pretrial preparation. (This will be discussed hereinafter.)

8. In certain circumstances, a written report may be obtained from the expert. (This will be discussed hereinafter.)

9. The expert may assist counsel in preparing his Medical Malpractice Panel Submission.

10. The expert may assist counsel in preparing for trial.

11. Direct testimony at trial for the purpose of establishing and/or supporting a *prima facie* case.

12. Rebuttal testimony.

Needless to say, possible uses of the medical expert are multiple and discretion must be used on a case by case basis. An important caveat is not to overuse the single expert in fields or areas beyond his expertise. An internist may have some familiarity with reviewing X-rays or pathology slides. It may, however, be quite pointful to obtain additional expert help in these areas. Many counsel are concerned with the prospect of mounting expenses by the repeated use of the medical-legal expert. Our only comment in this regard is that, of course, we too, have this same concern, and we try to use our discretion.

The bottom line, of course, is to attempt to choose cases which have the likely merit of justifying these expenses, and to recognize our obligation to do all that is reasonably necessary to advance our client's legitimate interests. We certainly cannot say that every dollar spent on every medical expert we have ever had has been "worth it." However, by and large, the money spent on our medical-legal experts has worked to the enormous benefit of our clients, and to ourselves.

V. PRETRIAL DEPOSITION OF PLAINTIFF'S MEDICAL EXPERT

New York CPLR sec. 3101 (a)(3) states in substance that regardless of burden of proof there shall be full disclosure of, among other things, a person ". . . who has been retained by him as an expert witness."

Therefore the plaintiff does have the option of pretrial deposition of his expert witness and this deposition may be used at trial to support the plaintiff's case.

In many states and in the Federal system, disclosure of the expert witness is required. At times the defense will wish to and have a right to depose the plaintiff's expert. Normally, the plaintiff would wish to resist such disclosure, if possible.

In the New York State Court system, the plaintiff is not required to disclose the expert. Then why would the plaintiff wish to voluntarily disclose the expert and subject said expert to questioning during the pretrial stage? The answer to this question is that in most instances, the plaintiff would not wish this method of disclosure. From a tactical point of view it is usually best to give the defense as little time and opportunity as possible as to "adjust" their defense to the expert's thrust.

Like all general rules, there are certain important and significant exceptions. The primary practical use of this method of disclosure would be the circumstance in which plaintiff's expert witness will not or might not be available at the time of trial. One might also envision circumstances in which a certain expert witness will actually sound better to a jury on paper, rather than "live." Of course it is possible to have this pretrial testimony on video tape. Plaintiff's counsel must take into account the question of expense in this regard.

We have twice employed this method of disclosure knowing that we had guaranteed certain almost "irreplacable" expert testimony for trial. We knew that in both instances that should it be necessary to read the deposition at trial, such testimony would be buttressed by certain other live testimony at trial, should such become necessary. A trial of an action without any live witness would be rather "dry," unexciting and probably unsuccessful.

In one instance, in which we produced a medical-legal expert for pretrial deposition, we had the unexpected but happy bonus of a defense attorney who quite frankly was unprepared for an in-depth cross-examination of the expert. This case was later settled for a substantial sum of money, prior even to the panel hearing. In the second instance, the expert's transcript was used to a great advantage at the medical malpractice panel, and the case was satisfactorily settled at the time of trial.

Effective for any action commenced on or after July 1, 1985, CPLR sec. 3101 has been recently amended to permit certain limited discovery of experts. "Discovery" of an adversary's expert witness is now obtainable "on request." As such, either side may make a demand for the adversary's expert. However, in a medical or dental malpractice action, a response to the expert demand may omit the name of the medical or dental expert. The responding party, however, is still required to disclose in "reasonable detail":

1. Subject matter of the expected expert testimony.

2. The substance of the facts and opinions of the expected testimony.

3. The qualification of the expert.

4. A summary of the grounds for each expert's opinion.

This new law permits either side to avoid the aforesaid disclosure provisions where appropriate notice cannot be given before trial if a party for "good cause" retains the expert an "insufficient period of time" prior to trial. This provision of law permits the trial court to exercise discretion in the interests of justice to avoid preclusion.

With a showing of "special circumstances," either side may obtain additional disclosure by court order. However, court order is not necessary to take pretrial testimony of a treating physician. It would appear as if the withholding of the expert's name would by implication preclude pretrial deposition of the adversary's medical expert in the absence of "special circumstances."

The practical implication of these new provisions of law are as follows:

1. The defendant will have a right to know in advance just which medical specialities will be used by the plaintiff to support the theory of liability.

2. The defendant in advance will have a more precise statement as to the plaintiff's theory of liability; furthermore, said expert's statement will be a further tool of defense cross-examination.

3. Similarly, the plaintiff will know in advance just which medical specialties the defense will produce; and similarly, the plaintiff will know in advance more precisely just what the defense experts will claim.

4. As such, the plaintiff will have additional responsibility in "preparation" of the medical experts. This additional "preparation" will include familiarizing the expert with the pretrial statement attributed to him or her so that said expert may comfortably deal with such should it be raised on cross-examination. Additionally, the expert should be prepared to deal with the medical propositions that are likely to be advanced by defense experts. The defendant's preparation, on the other hand, may still employ a "wait and see" posture as the plaintiff must go first at the actual trial.

VI. MEDICAL-LEGAL EXPERT'S WRITTEN REPORT

The question arises as to whether plaintiff's counsel wants or needs a written report from the expert, and if so, what should be included within the report. In many states, a written report from plaintiff's expert which must be exchanged with the adversary, is required. Such a report may be required in the Federal system. In New York State there is no requirement to obtain a written report and therefore it is our feeling that such ordinarily should not be obtained by the plaintiff, except for the type of report to be used with the malpractice panel submission as referred to hereinafter. Whatever interview is had between plaintiff's counsel and medical-legal expert, and whatever notes are taken by plaintiff's counsel would of course be "attorney work product" and therefore not subject to discovery.

It is generally our feeling that an expert's report should be obtained and made part of the plaintiff's medical malpractice panel submission. In general, it is our view that said expert's report should be brief, conclusory in nature and essentially to the point of supporting the merit of the plaintiff's case. The details of the case should be included in the plaintiff's panel submission. In our view, the purpose of the report is merely to demonstrate that indeed the plaintiff does have at least one qualified expert supporting the case. By in large, the decision of the panel would turn on the medical member's view of the case. If the medical panelist believes that there is merit to the case, then the likelihood of a finding for the plaintiff is great—regardless of whether there is or is not an expert's report attached. On the other hand, if the medical panelist's view of the plaintiff's case is negative, then the success of the panel will be achieved by a "no finding." It is in this latter circumstance where the value of the report comes in. At least in our own view the presence of a report takes the Judge and Attorney-Panelist "off the hook." Should the Panel Justice and/or the Panel Attorney believe that there is merit to the plaintiff's case or at least a "question of fact," then they can merely point out that there is a dispute among the experts and that the matter should properly be left to the trial without any panel finding.

The potential problem with the written report is that it may be used by defense counsel during trial to cross-examine your expert. Shrewd defense counsel will look through the report to see if they can determine some inconsistency between the facts and/or medical principles contained in the report with those presented at trial. They will look for certain medical facts which are not included in the report and attempt to demonstrate that the expert formed a conclusion without full knowledge of what was truly involved. Therefore, when a medical report is prepared, it is encumbent upon plaintiff's counsel to be sufficiently familiar with all of the records and facts in the case so that the expert may not be impeached or embarrassed at the time of trial—even on what truly may be inconsequential or irrelevant collateral items.

As with most sophisticated and successful dealings with experts, the question of an expert's report is one that requires forethought, common sense, preparation, and total knowledge of the case.

VII. PAYING THE MEDICAL-LEGAL EXPERT

The issue of payment revolves around questions of credibility and budget. As previously referred to, payment is essential and frequently substantial because of substantial input required of the medical-legal expert. While we have the usual concerns of any other plaintiff's firm with regard to mounting pretrial expenses, we recognize that in order to be successful, this is not a place to "skimp." One must be concerned with the issue of credibility. Frankly, experts who are receiving large sums for their services may be viewed by the jury as witnesses who are not credible. It goes without saying that under no circumstance may an expert be compensated on a "contingency." Should such a circumstance be brought out at the time of trial, it is our view that the expert is virtually worthless as a credible witness.

Generally, it is our view that if a medical-legal expert is charging at approximately the same rate as for his professional services in clinical medicine, the jury will accept such a circumstance as reasonable. At first blush, $150 to $200 per hour may seem enormous to the average juror who may not be making that much more for a full 40-hour week. Yet if this amount is what doctors are receiving per hour for clinical work, then it surely is not the fault of the plaintiff that doctors are making so much money per hour. Clearly this is a matter to be discussed openly and honestly with the expert, so that the responses at trial will appear natural and reasonable.

VIII. PREPARING THE MEDICAL EXPERT FOR DIRECT EXAMINATION

Preparing plaintiff's expert for direct examination, at first blush, is such an obvious requirement of any plaintiff's attorney that perhaps not much need to be said in this regard. It goes without saying that the attorney must learn of and be prepared to develop the expert's qualifications, establish certain medical facts and principles, and establish a *prima facie* case.

Often plaintiff's counsel will obtain a copy of the expert's curriculum vitae, and merely run through such with the expert at the time of trial. This, however, may be quite boring, particularly if the expert is announcing every society he is a member of and/or every paper he has written. It is important that the medical-legal expert does not come across as "pompous." The first thing that the plaintiff's counsel may wish to consider is "what is special about this expert?" The expert may have written, studied or had special practical training or experience in the particular area at issue in the case. Plaintiff's counsel may wish to emphasize this circumstance. The expert witness may have certain special experience in training and/or teaching physicians and medical students. Certainly, in this capacity, the expert may be eminently qualified to set forth the "standard of care." It may well be that there is really nothing "special" about this particular expert witness. Rather, the expert may be just another hard working physician who day-in and day-out is responsible for patient care. This expert may then be presented in light of being the "average" physician who recognizes just what the standards are for similarly situated "average" physicians. The announcement of a standard of care and a departure from such by an "average" medical-legal expert may well be quite potent, in the right circumstance.

In the New York State Courts, a hypothetical question is generally not required. We prefer not to use the hypothetical question. It goes without saying that the expert should be fully familiar with all of the medical and hospital records. The ideal situation is for the expert also to be familiar with both pretrial testimony as well as previous trial testimony of other medical witnesses. This not only would include testimony from the defendants but also any previously employed medical expert for the plaintiff.

There should be a full discussion with the medical expert concerning the importance of phrasing of both questions and answers, particularly with respect to the subject of "proximate cause." The medical expert should be alerted to the problem that will arise if he is careless or slovenly in his language. If the expert uses such phrases as "possible," "maybe," "could be" or any similar type verbiage, problems will ensue. Plaintiff, of course, does not have to establish a departure from a standard of care and damages on the basis of an absolute certainty. A reasonable or substantial probability is sufficient.

On the other hand, the expert should be cautioned not to oversell or be too strong in his language. We generally like to avoid use of the phrase "guilty." An expert's statement that a defendant is "guilty of reckless and gross negligence" is a type of overkill that in many instances may cause the jury to believe that this expert is not objective. The passwords are "reasonable, calm moderation." Hopefully, the jury will believe that the expert is knowledgeable, sensible, practical, and indeed even fair to the defendant.

Plaintiff's counsel should also give serious consideration to the use of demonstrative evidence. A model and/or diagram may be quite helpful in the presentation and explanation. If the jury is able to follow along and understand just what it is the expert is saying, then they are far more likely to believe what the expert is testifying to.

IX. PREPARING THE MEDICAL EXPERT FOR CROSS-EXAMINATION

This is perhaps the area in which plaintiff's counsel requires the greatest use of his skill and the area which may reap the greatest of dividends.

It is often said by experienced trial counsel that all expert witnesses sound great on direct examination but that the true test is how they stand up under cross-examination. We generally concur in this concept.

How does one prepare the expert witness for the adversary's cross-examination when you do not know just what it is that the adversary will ask? The answer to this question is that in most instances and in most areas astute plaintiff's trial counsel should be able to figure out what it is that his adversary will ask on cross-examination. If plaintiff's expert has testified in the past there should be a thorough discussion as to just what type of inquiries this expert has been subjected to. Be prepared for defense counsel producing a transcript of this expert's prior testimony. Has this expert ever testified on the subject matter of the case at bar? If so what has he said on this subject? If the expert has testified on the subject of the case, but in the context of a different fact pattern, that expert should be thoroughly prepared to appropriately respond if challenged by what appears to be contradictory testimony.

In the New York State Court system, medical literature may not be used affirmatively to buttress the expert's testimony. Such literature may be affirmatively used by plaintiff's expert in the Federal Court system. Frequently, defense counsel will confront the expert with a book or article and ask if such is viewed by the expert as authoritative. If the expert does recognize the book or article as authoritative, then for impeachment purposes a passage from the book or article which is inconsistent with said expert's testimony, may be read.

We view the area of possible cross-examination with medical literature as an important subject of trial preparation. It should be explained to the expert that he may be confronted with this literature only if the expert recognizes the material as authoritative. Some medical experts refuse to recognize anything as authoritative. Generally, we are not happy with this approach. The expert may well come across as appearing "arrogant," not to recognize anyone else as authoritative. Knowing all of the relevant and significant literature in advance may well produce great dividends for your expert on cross-examination. If the expert knows in advance what is in the literature and how to deal with that literature in the context of the case at bar, cross-examination on this subject may well be successfully diverted in favor of the plaintiff. An expert who is not only independently knowledgeable on the medical subject matter of the case, but who also appears to be thoroughly familiar with the relevant literature and willing to discuss same with adversary counsel may appear even more credible.

We have had the following type of circumstance develop in many cases:

Q: Doctor, do you recognize *Smith's Textbook on Gastroenterology* as being an authority?

A: Well, I don't know that I would consider it to be an authority but I do know the book and I would be happy to discuss it with you.

(Plunging on, defense counsel may feel that plaintiff's counsel is sleeping when not interposing an objection to the following question.)

Q: Do you agree with the following statement: "Cancer of the stomach is invariably fatal, with only the smallest percentage surviving more than five years?"

A: I am familiar with that statement, would you like my comments on that?

Q: No, Doctor, I ask you if you agree or disagree with that statement, since that statement is inconsistent with what you have given on your direct testimony?

A: I beg to differ with you, sir, that statement is not inconsistent with what I have said on my direct testimony. That is a statement that you have taken out of context. I would be happy to discuss it with you. As I told you before I am familiar with that literature.

Q: Doctor, do you mean to say that you cannot answer my question yes or no? Do you agree or disagree with that statement?

A: Sir, I would like to answer your question. As I said before the context within that book, in which that statement exists, I generally agree with. As I said before it is not inconsistent with what I've said on direct examination. I surely would be happy to explain if you would give me the opportunity.

Q: So, Doctor, you persist in not answering my question. You cannot say whether you agree or disagree?

A: Well, I am sorry that I have not been able to communicate a better answer to you. I think I have answered your question, at least to the best of my ability.

Please note in this type of exchange, plaintiff's counsel, having thoroughly prepared his witness, has remained on the sidelines and stayed out of the exchange. Defense counsel has not scored any points. On the contrary, defense counsel himself may have come across poorly. Having anticipated this cross-examination, plaintiff's expert is calm, relaxed and knowledgeable. He is willing to discuss the statement. He is not disagreeing with the book, he merely would like to place the statement in context. If not given the opportunity to "explain" on this cross-examination, at times the trial judge will intercede and ask the witness to "explain" and plaintiff's counsel may on redirect do the following:

Q: Doctor, on several occasions during cross-examination you expressed a desire to discuss the context in which the statement from *Smith's on Gastroenterology* was presented to you; would you kindly explain that to the jury?

A: Certainly. The statement that was read from that textbook generally referred to a circumstance in which there already had been metastatic spread to the regional lymph nodes. It is this metastatic spread that we wish to avoid by early diagnosis and surgical treatment. Therefore in that context I do not disagree with that statement. In this case, however, I believe that the eight- to nine-month delay in diagnosis of the stomach tumor permitted this metastatic spread. Based on my knowledge of this type of tumor, it is my opinion that it is highly probable that timely diagnosis and treatment would have resulted in surgical removal of the tumor before metastatic spread. The natural progression of this disease does not mean that from its beginning to its end it is invariably fatal. I think it unfair to suggest that this patient was doomed from the beginning and it is my conviction that this patient was deprived of a substantial and reasonable opportunity for cure.

A very important rule for both plaintiff's counsel and expert, during the cross-examination of the adversary, is to be patient and nonargumentative. The expert should be instructed that if the form of the question limits thc answer, that said expert should confine the answer to the prescribed limits with knowledge that an explanation will be possible on redirect examination.

If the witness cannot answer a question "yes" or "no" the witness should say so. The witness should not try to blurt out or get in certain answers that are not called for. The witness should try to avoid an antagonistic "wrestling match" with adversary counsel. You want your witness to come off as being knowledgeable, calm, professional and honest. There are questions that can and indeed must be answered yes or no. Even if this may appear for the moment to leave something hanging out of context or perhaps misleading—let it go. Let your expert know in advance that you will tie up these loose ends on redirect. Let your expert feel comfortable with these answers. Anticipate these type of questions so that your expert will know that there is no need to argue with the cross-examiner.

One expert we know was being badgered on cross-examination repeatedly to answer certain questions yes or no. These same type questions were being asked over and over again. The judge turned to the expert: "Why can't you answer that question yes or no?" The expert responded, "Your Honor, I feel like a witness being shown a circle and being asked if this is a square or a triangle. Being shown a circle I would like the opportunity to answer that it is a circle."

Perhaps the key to the successful interaction between plaintiff's counsel and his expert in successfully blunting the cross-examination is to be working on the same wave lengths. Some experts feel threatened by collateral attack and sometimes respond in anger and/or by volunteering many items not asked. This may lead the jury to feel that the expert has something to hide. Why the overreaction? We have had occasion where our expert has been asked if he had testified on many prior occasions for our firm, on each of which occasions he was paid. The expert responded that indeed he had testified a number of times for our firm and had been paid well on each of those occasions. The expert answered these questions in a relaxed, nonantagoinistic matter of fact way without volunteering anything further. However, on redirect examination the expert was asked the following series of questions:

Q: Sir, on cross-examination, reference was made to the fact that your medical knowledge and expertise were required by our law firm on a number of prior occasions. Do you recall that?

A: I recall that testimony.

Q: Is our firm the only law firm that has ever requested your services as a medical expert?

A: No, sir.

Q: Has the law firm of defense counsel ever asked you to advise them and their clients on medical-legal subjects?

A: Yes, as a matter of fact on many occasions.

Q: Doctor, have you always given them your honest opinion?

A: I have.

Q: And have they paid you on each and every occasion when they sought your services?

A: They have.

Q: Doctor, when we have consulted you in the past have you always given us your honest opinion?

A: I certainly have.

Q: Doctor, have there been times in the past when we have consulted you and asked you about the merits of a case in which you have advised us that you did not believe that there was merit to our case?

A: That is true.

Q: Have you ever testified for us in a case in which you did not believe the case had merit?

A: Absolutely not.

It is generally our feeling that if defense counsel does not embark on a collateral attack of our expert, that there is no reason to bolster the credibility of said expert by eliciting the aforesaid type of questioning. On the other hand, it seems to us that any collateral attack could only be for the purpose of suggesting to the jury that this expert witness is not testifying truthfully and honestly. That collateral attack in our view opens up the circumstance that said expert has been consulted by various defense counsel, by various hospitals and doctors, and perhaps even by the defense counsel defending the case at bar.

On cross-examination of plaintiff's expert, both form and substance are critical. It is self-evident that the expert must not yield a *prima facie* case on cross-examination, otherwise plaintiff's case will not survive.

In this latter regard, plaintiff's expert should be carefully prepared on the difference between "judgment" and "standard of care," and the difference between "possible" and "probable." Plaintiff's expert should readily concede that doctors frequently exercise their judgment. The expert should be prepared to explain why the act or omission of the defendant in the case at bar was not an exercise of judgment. Pointfully, plaintiff's counsel should have his expert understand that judgment may be exercised only after there is a careful examination and evaluation. The doing or not doing of a careful examination or evaluation is not "judgmental."

Furthermore the exercise of judgment may only be within the framework of a recognized standard modality of therapy. For example, it is not an exercise of judgment to leave a patient unattended. Leaving a patient unattended may or may not be deviation from the standard of care depending upon the circumstances.

In terms of the "proximate cause" issue, the expert should be prepared to deal with the concept of "possible" versus "probable." Experts should be prepared to concede that "anything is possible."

Q: Doctor, isn't it equally possible that this injury would have occurred regardless of the acts of the defendants in this case?

A: Anything is possible, but I do not agree with what you say. On the contrary, I think it unlikely that this injury would have occurred had there been timely diagnosis. I think it probable the injury would not have occurred had there been timely diagnosis. I would be happy to explain my reasons again.

This latter response is clearly one of "holding the line" and is not only positive for the plaintiff in substance, but also is presented in a highly credible manner.

A final point for consideration is that no matter how plaintiff's counsel is preparing his expert for cross-examination, it must be recognized that "personalities" are involved. There are some experts who are just going to go their own way no matter what you tell them. Sometimes plaintiff's counsel must accept the "good with the bad." There are times in which one cannot afford the luxury of avoiding using the expert or getting a different expert. However, if an expert who is likely to handle himself poorly on cross-examination, regardless of preparation, is not necessary to the plaintiff's case, then it goes without saying that the expert should not be used.

X. REDIRECT EXAMINATION

We have previously made reference to the use of redirect examination to tie up loose ends and/or allow your expert to explain that which has been obstructed on cross-examination. We have found redirect examination properly used may at times neutralize an entire cross-examination attack. In one case, our obstetrical expert testified that it was a departure from the standard of care to stimulate labor where a baby was known to be in a face position. On cross-examination the expert was asked if reputable physicians had ever used labor stimulation with a known face position and he agreed that many had. He further recognized medical literature describing a proper stimulation of labor with a known face position. Left hanging, this cross-examination seemed to have devastated the expert's testimony. This literature and cross-examination were anticipated and dealt with as follows on redirect examination:

Q: Doctor, are you familiar with that literature read to you by defense counsel?

A: I am.

Q: What is that literature referring to?

A: It was referring to the use of labor stimulation with a face position where the baby was known to be premature.

Q: Is that the same situation as in this case?

A: No, it is not.

Q: Can you explain that for us?

A: Certainly. As I explained earlier, the reason for a face position is that for some reason the size of the mother's birth canal and the size of the baby's head are not compatible, thereby permitting this abnormal position. With premature babies, the birth canal is too large and the head is too small. And it is this lack of accommodation that permits the face position. If you know the baby is small in comparison to the birth canal then obviously there is no danger in forcing the baby through the birth canal as indeed there is ample room for the face position to correct itself during labor. On the other hand, as in this case, we know that the baby was very large and that there was no prematurity. Therefore, in advance we know that the likely reason for the face position is that the head is too large for the birth canal. It is in this instance that it would be contrary to good practice to try to force the head through. Since not only can this abnormal position not be corrected, but the mother and baby may be harmed in the meantime.

This type of redirect examination is devastating. What the witness has now explained makes sense. More importantly it exposes the defense to what the jury may interpret as "shoddy" practice. The cross-examination is actually misleading.

Many experienced trial attorneys breathe a sigh of relief when their expert leaves the witness stand with a *prima facie* case intact. Surely discretion must be used in terms of redirect examination. Further redirect examination exposes your expert to further cross-examination. Obviously, judgment, experience and trial developments must dictate to what extent, if at all, this redirect examination may be employed.

XI. PREPARATION FOR REBUTTAL TESTIMONY

The plaintiff has a right to bring in rebuttal testimony essentially to rebut new matters or concepts raised by the defense. Allowing this testimony is to a large degree discretionary with the Court, the issue being whether or not the proposed rebuttal testimony is a reiteration—a last word effort by the plaintiff. In some cases, the need for rebuttal testimony is obvious and essential. In one case that comes to mind, the defense not only disputed our contentions concerning the standard of care, but produced copies of certain X-rays which allegedly refuted our contention on the issue of proximate cause. On our rebuttal case, we produced the radiologist with the original X-rays and in addition a separate radiological expert. This latter circumstance involved two independent witnesses who had not previously been involved in the case. There are times, of course, when one may wish to recall an expert who has testified as part of the direct case for the purpose of rebutting an item raised by the defense. At times this has worked to great advantage. However, we can recall one instance when at least one juror, who had previously been impressed by our expert on the direct case, had a change of heart at least concerning this particular expert when he reappeared on rebuttal.

XII. CONCLUSION

In the preceeding pages, we have set forth very few mandates or unbreakable rules. Most of the strategy and work will be dependant upon counsel's experience, judgment, common sense, and case by case circumstances and developments. Hopefully, we have called to the attention of trial counsel multiple areas that will set the thinking aparatus in motion. The only real unshakeable and unyielding rule is that counsel must know his case in depth and be prepared to devote unstinting effort and energy to the subject of "obtaining, preparing and using the expert medical witness."

CHAPTER THIRTEEN

THEORY AND STRATEGY IN MEDICAL MALPRACTICE CASES

Harvey Weitz, Esq.

Despite the frequently voiced lamentations to the effect that enormous jury verdicts have prompted a "malpractice" crisis, the fact is that the vast majority of medical malpractice trials end in verdicts **in favor of the defendant**. The medical profession offers a facile explanation for this sober statistic. It claims that most cases are without medical merit. Is this allegation correct? These statistics and claims caused this writer to undertake an analysis of a number of reported cases which resulted in defense verdicts although major and even catastrophic injuries were involved. The conclusions reached are not based on statistical analysis, but rather on a case by case examination of the facts and claims of all parties.

In essence, it is this writer's opinion that the high mortality rate for plaintiffs' cases is best explained by the failure of the plaintiff's counsel to **focus** on a **specific** medical event which not only is indicative of malpractice, but also demonstrates that the treatment was a substantial factor in producing a new injury or in allowing the persistence of an otherwise curable problem. Too often the plaintiff's attorney is his own worst enemy; instead of focusing on the issue which will win his case, he cannot resist stressing other areas of treatment which, whether or not indicative of malpractice, had nothing to do with the ultimate injury for which the plaintiff seeks compensation.

When a medical malpractice trial follows a convoluted and complex course, it will ordinarily result in a defendant's verdict; this is true notwithstanding the brilliance of counsel and his adroit trial tactics. Jurors are reasonable persons who respond to logic and morality. A sound and straightforword theory of liability produces a winning case.

I. THE OBJECTIVES OF THEORY SELECTION

If plaintiff's counsel wants to prevent his case from becoming another negative statistic, he must draw a plain and precise theory of liability which will serve two purposes. First, it must meet the plaintiff's burden of persuasion. Second, it must preempt the anticipated defense.

II. AVOIDING THE PITFALLS

Since medicine is not an exact science, it is not unusual in any single case to find a number of departures from good and standard medical practice. Here lies the major trap for inexperienced counsel. All too often substantial time and money are spent on developing the various elements of an apparent deviation, which, however egregious, did not cause the poor medical result. For example, standing alone, a nurse's failure to give the proper dosage of an antibiotic does not establish a legally sufficient cause of action. Similarly, some untimely execution of a doctor's order or the injudicious use of medication or the failure to chart a patient's vital signs do not, of themselves, suffice to create liability. From a tactical viewpoint, these departures have their place in the trial, but they should divert neither counsel nor the jury from focusing on the theory of the case. Today's "victory" over a nurse's failure to chart his actions may affect his credibility, but two weeks later it will not carry the day in the jury deliberation room. Demonstrative evidence, trial tactics, and evidence of substandard care all are useful at trial, **but the jury's attention must be focused on the issue counsel wishes to be dispositive at trial**. It is the overall strategy as dictated by the case theory which will produce a plaintiff's verdict.

The doctor's general competence, the adequacy of his training, his lack of experience, his lack of attentiveness or even his good faith all are **collateral** matters which serve to divert the jury's attention from the theory of the case. The plaintiff's burden is sufficiently difficult without the need to increase that burden by anything which smacks of television soap opera. In an appropriate case, the jury, on its own, will bring to bear its moral outrage—**but only after it accepts the liability theory**. The typical case does not involve outrageous conduct by the physicians or the hospital staff. Usually, you will face an experienced, well-trained physician who will testify with great conviction as to the care and concern he exercised in treating the patient. Thus, it is essential to develop the liability theory which enables you to argue simply that a mistake has been made, and that, just as an experienced, good driver might make a careless wide turn causing injury, an experienced, good doctor, may commit an error which causes injury. Framing the dispute in this fashion imposes an understandable and appropriately modest burden of persuasion.

III. THEORY SELECTION

Theory selection rests upon two elemental concepts common to all litigation—the facts and the law. First, there must be a comprehensive assemblage of all the facts. **No source of information may be safely overlooked**. Counsel must investigate all the available medical records and conduct in-depth interviews with the patient and his family. The admonition of

Sir William Moseley to his medical students serves the lawyer equally well. Sir William said: "Listen to the patient; he is giving you the diagnosis." In many cases, a detailed history of the symptomatology is critical. Every attorney practicing in the medical malpractice field knows how often a hospital "blows a case" because of a house physician's failure to elicit a good history. The plaintiff's lawyer must profit from this example and spend every minute or hour necessary to draw out every scrap of information known to the patient, his family and, sometimes, even visitors. This information together with documentary material (hospital records, physician's charts, medical reports, laboratory findings, work records and the like) then should be fashioned into a simple jargon-free chronological narrative which allows anyone to understand the sequence of events. Not until this is accomplished may one undertake a retrospective examination of the medical result to determine its cause.

Second, plaintiff's counsel must reorient his thinking as to what the law means by "medical malpractice." The concept of malpractice is rather simple. It does not demand the highest degree of skill and care. Rather, it merely asks the medical practitioner to provide ordinary, good and accepted medical care. The phrase "malpractice" is a pejorative term which tends to enhance and increase plaintiff's burden of proof. Dramatists have distorted the term so that the public has come to view it as something akin to an immoral act or as a hearing to determine the doctor's right to practice medicine. Counsel should bear in mind that **a deviation from good practice is a mistake which may be made by any highly competent physician**. The typical case involves a physician who knew better, who had the fund of knowledge, who had the skills required, but who failed for one reason or another to exercise his skill and knowledge. Attempting to impune the expertise of the physician usually leads counsel astray and causes the case to be fought on the wrong grounds.

For example, the use of Pitocin for the doctor's convenience is deplorable medical practice, but it is the dangerous nature of Pitocin which must be established. Having another patient in labor or wanting to leave for the golf course helps explain the circumstances, but the focus of the case must be on the *dangerous* and *unnecessary* use of the drug. Good medical practice demands a sound medical reason for the use of a drug. That is the theory. However elementary this admonition, plaintiff's counsel must bear in mind his primary goal is to win the case. Damages will come as a natural consequence of winning; turning the trial into a morality play in order to enhance damages risks losing the case for a gain which is an inevitable concomitant of victory.

Thus, in theory development, we look first for a single **simple issue**, and second, for an issue which will preempt the typical malpractice defenses. In the usual case, it will not be overly difficult to anticipate the general tenor, if not the specifics, of the defense.

Every good defense counsel will seek to portray his negligent doctor as a "good" person who struggled day and night against overwhelming odds to bring his patient through, but that, in spite of these Herculean efforts and self-sacrifice, the "fates" were against the plaintiff and the poor outcome was inevitable. In virtually every case of negligent treatment there is, of course, an underlying illness. In many of these cases, it is impossible to demonstrate that proper treatment inevitably would have resulted in a cure. The defense will place great emphasis on the gravity of the patient's situation and the difficulties facing the doctor. Defense counsel will paint a picture of a patient at death's door and a doctor struggling to salvage the patient's life in spite of the impossible odds. The doctrine of preemption requires that these realities be taken into account in developing the case theory.

Thus, in a claim of negligent treatment, the theory must focus on the objectives of the treatment, the doctor's ability to provide this care **and the proven past effectiveness of the proper treatment**. After all, that is the raison d'etre of medical practice and that is why the doctor undertook to treat the patient. Defense counsel will claim that his client is a hard-working, experienced and thorough physician, but that he is not a guarantor of success. We may turn this defense to our advantage by extrapolating from the doctor's experience and knowledge that he was familiar with and capable of providing the proper treatment. The average physician will proudly declaim that he keeps current in the medical literature, that he attends continuing medical education programs, and that he regularly attends the staff conferences at his hospital. In this manner, we often are able to extract from him/her an admission that the method of treatment plaintiff alleges should have been rendered is an acknowledged, viable, appropriate and acceptable method of treatment. We may narrow the issues further by directing ourselves as to why the treatment selected by the defendant was contraindicated in our case. Or we may choose to demonstrate that the method of treatment selected by the defendant carried with it the substantial risk of causing the very injury suffered by the plaintiff, while the alternate methods did not.

In the negligent diagnosis case, we have a similar problem of an underlying illness. The usual defense is "mere error of judgment." Frequently, defense counsel is able to present several disease entities which might account for plaintiff's condition, including the condition diagnosed by the defendant. All too often plaintiff's expert is apt to concede that his judgment is a retrospective view and that the defendant's judgment was consistent with the clinical procedure. The best theory in such a situation is the failure to make a differential diagnosis.

The defendant physician will not want to appear ignorant. We can be sure that the defendant doctor, given the opportunity, will be proud to explain the breadth and depth of his medical knowledge. He certainly will not quarrel with the proposition that it was his obligation to rule out those diseases which were consistent with the clinical picture presented by the patient and in order of their severity, thereby admitting the necessity for making a differential diagnosis. If he failed to make a differential diagnosis, he would perforce be culpable of malpractice. If he claims to have considered various possible diagnoses, he is then required to rule out all but the condition which is the cause of the plaintiff's problem. Usually the medical work-up required to complete a differential diagnosis is well-known and routine, and thus we attempt to focus in on the failure to take those tests which would rule out the inapplicable diagnoses and rule in the actual diagnosis. Of course, the variables of time and severity of condition must be factored into the testing procedure. But the keystone of the liability theory is the doctor's obligation to make a differential diagnosis. Since the poor outcome bespeaks the true diagnosis, the jury should have no trouble understanding why the doctor's failure caused the injury.

IV. CONCLUSION

It has often been said that defense counsel is the one who determines whether a jury will decide a case. Usually it is within his power to dispose of the case by proffering a reasonable offer to the plaintiff. The cases which go to the jury most often are those involving negligent diagnosis or a wrong choice of treatment or those which depend on credibility of the plaintiff's version of the facts. In this paper, we have presented an approach to theory selection which does not rely on the plaintiff's credibility, but instead involves **acceptance of the defendant's knowledge and expertise**, and the use of those factors as the basis for the claim against him.

CHAPTER FOURTEEN

PLAINTIFF'S JURY SELECTION

Harry H. Lipsig, Esq.

I. HELPLESSNESS OF PATIENT

The key to a plaintiff's verdict in a medical malpractice case is the underlying theme that I always enunciate and which should be used right from the *voir dire* itself to almost the last sentence in summation. It is a theme that hits the possible unperceived worry of everyone, more particularly when they have to undergo operations and anesthesiological procedures.

This theme is that the patient is, in many instances, helpless in the hands of the doctor or surgeon, and is unable to be aware of anything that would save him from possible misadventure.

Anyone who is due to be operated on is bound to have the conscious or subconscious thought, "My goodness, I am likely to die and never even know I am dying. Will I live to see the light of day again?" The extent of this feeling, whether casual or otherwise, is rarely fully realized.

I was dramatically made aware of this when I was first operated on. I was very casual as to the operation, having made arrangements to go to the theater the night before, but the hospital intake nurse cancelled that.

At the very moment of awakening from the operation, I was suffused with the exultant feeling, "I am here! I am alive!" It was then that I was brought face to face with what had been an unrecognized, subconscious fear.

Accordingly, after asking jurors the various routine questions, I then ask them, "Have you ever had to contemplate being operated on and been worried about the fact that you would be asleep from the anesthesia and helpless to avoid any carelessness on the part of the doctors into whose care you have entrusted your life? Have you at any time felt helpless when you have entrusted yourself into the care of a doctor for treatment?"

By asking this, you are highlighting for each juror the helplessness of the patient in the care of the doctor and the superior position of the doctor. You are sparking a fear for himself against the spectre of the risks of being in any doctor's care.

II. PHYSICIAN PROPAGANDA

Of course, today the question of whether or not jurors have been affected by the doctors' propaganda should be dug into in preparation to whatever extent necessary in each locality. Accordingly, ask the prospective jurors, "Have you been subjected to any of the propaganda of doctors in medical malpractice cases?"

Notice the word "subjected." That gives a tinge to the propaganda. One might ask, "Have you been subjected to the publicity and propaganda that doctors have been putting forth." Probe the jury on the extent of its influence.

One might also put it another way, with proper tone of phrase, satirically, "I, of course, don't think the doctors have deliberately designed this propaganda to affect juries' viewpoints. In any event, have you been subjected to, or otherwise become aware of, these campaigns by doctors?"

Others may disagree, but I hesitate to mention some of their themes, especially the item of increased cost of medical care by reason of malpractice claims, for the same reason that one doesn't mention a competitor's product.

If there is the slightest possibility that defense counsel is likely to try to parade any of the propaganda claims made by doctors, an application should be made to the Court, prior to the jury selection, to limit defense counsel. One should never gamble by failing to make these motions *in limine*, for a whole panel can be poisoned.

III. JURORS' ATTITUDES TOWARD DOCTORS

Questions should be asked as to how cordial jurors feel toward their doctors. On finding such relations and eliciting affirmative information in this direction, one should uncover to what extent the friendliness would carry over to other doctors, such as the defendant's.

IV. JURORS' KNOWLEDGE OF DOCTORS IN CASE

The more closely knit the community is, the more thorough should be the questions as to the jurors having any awareness of any of the doctors in the case, going right through the whole list and not merely the outstanding defendants, including doctors one would anticipate might be called as witnesses by the other side.

Of course, there are the more obvious questions such as:

1. Whether the jurors or their immediate families have any relations or have any contact of any consequence with hospitals, doctors, osteopaths, chiropractors, podiatrists, therapists, nurses, and finally with health care providers of any kind.

2. Whether or not they feel that a doctor is clothed with a greater halo of truth than other humans.

3. Do any of them place a doctor upon any sort of pedestal?

4. Do any of them feel that doctors don't make mistakes or that they are perfect human beings? (That should bring a smile.) Putting a light touch on it, one might, in the proper atmosphere, follow up by daring to say, "After all, the truth is that you ladies and gentlemen of the jury and we lawyers are the only perfect people."

5. "Is there anybody on the jury who has ever found the perfect doctor?" might, under proper circumstances, be tested out for possible further discussions.

6. "Do you feel in this case the question of the doctors' reputation has anything to do with this case?" The doctors' ultimate standing or reputation is not an issue that should be involved in this case where we are concerned with the one problem of whether or not the doctors did or did not depart from proper medical procedure.

7. "Do you have any feeling that any such subject as the doctors' standing or reputation in the future should have anything to do with the situation between my client and the doctors, where the only problem is whether they acted properly or not?"

8. Whether they, or any member of their family, own or have owned any stock in, are or have been connected with, or in any manner interested in any insurance company issuing policies for protection against liability for damages.

The foregoing would seem to be the highlights, and modifications on them can be made according to each individual practitioner's own particular views. Questions in other directions can also be added as one considers necessary.

V. CROSS-EXAMINATION OF PHYSICIAN

For me, the underlying psychological thought is always, "We are helpless in the hands of the doctors to whom we entrust ourselves and you the jury surely often worry about the fact that you are in their hands." I carry this into cross-examination very often by asking the doctor questions that really answer themselves:

"Doctor 'Mary Sickly' came to you for *your* expertise, isn't that so?"

"Didn't 'Mary' come to you because she felt you knew the subject?"

"When 'Mary' was anesthetized, she was helpless and subject to your activities, was she not?"

Of course, with children I use the phraseology, "The child, Susan, could do nothing for herself."

Plaintiffs' full names should be sufficiently used in connection with questions to a point where one can slip into using only the plaintiff's first name, creating an acquaintanceship bond between the jury and the client. With children, having once mentioned the full name, I use the first name exclusively thereafter.

VI. TYPES OF JURORS DEPENDENT UPON TYPE OF CASE

One should bear in mind that for different medical problems one needs different types of jurors. In general, the older the juror the greater probability of the juror's knowledge of a doctor's fallibility based on the greater number of times that juror may have been subject to the treatment and error of doctors with corresponding less awe.

VII. SUMMARY

So, do remember, you are to flush out the underlying self-concern of every juror, through your genius, by causing him to visualize himself helpless and subject to the carefulness or possible carelessness of the everyday human being, the doctor. You can cause him to fret within himself over all of the risks that flow from being subject to another human being's possible failings.

Trial success is highly proportionate to what you accomplish in this regard, and its for you to find ways of furthering this underlying theme beyond the humble limits of what has been suggested herein.

You can do it!

CHAPTER FIFTEEN

DEFENDANT'S JURY SELECTION

Ernest F. W. Wildermuth, Jr., Esq.

I. INTRODUCTION

You represent the defendant doctor in a medical malpractice suit.

You have received and examined the summons and complaint, and have served a notice to state the amount sued for and find that plaintiff seeks ten million dollars. You further ascertain that the doctor's total insurance coverage is one million dollars.

You have reviewed, at length, the hospital chart and the doctor's office records, with the doctor.

You have reviewed the plaintiff's bill of particulars with your client and he has told you that, although its recitation of the final resulting physical condition of the plaintiff is correct (and it is not a good final physical condition), that condition is not as a result of any medical malpractice on his part. He explains to you the medical reason for the bad result of his treatment, and how it was unavoidable in this case.

You have consulted with medical experts and have been informed that, in their opinion, there has been no departure from good and accepted medical practice by your client in the treatment of his patient, and that what is complained of by plaintiff is simply an unfortunate medical result. It occurred for the same reasons that your client has already given you. You are told that the case is medically defensible.

You have attended all examinations before trial, and conducted other routine discovery procedures.

You have prepared contentions for the medical malpractice panel on behalf of the doctor, having all during the course of the development of the case read the necessary medical writings on the subject matter of your case.

You have appeared before the medical malpractice panel, and while the members seemed friendly and sympathetic to your arguments, and not quite receptive to the arguments of plaintiff's counsel, they have made no recommendations as to liability or no liability. You now know that neither you nor the plaintiff's counsel will be able to introduce the finding of the panel at the trial of the case.

You have become aware that the settlement demand of plaintiff's lawyer is within your client's total coverage, and you also know that an injury such as plaintiff has sustained has, in the past, brought jury verdicts considerably in excess of the doctor's coverage.

The case has worked its way up the trial calendar and the day comes when you are directed to select a jury.

II. THE SELECTION

In all probability, there will be codefendants in the case. The hospital where your client treated the plaintiff will be one, and there will probably be one or two remotely involved physicians. All of your prior research and investigation, however, indicates to one and all that if the plaintiff establishes a departure from good medical practice which caused the condition that plaintiff complains of, it will have been a departure by your client. This being the case, it is advisable for you to work out an understanding with the other defendants' lawyers, the course you have decided to pursue in jury selection, since you are the "target." It is desirable that there be no contradictions among defendants' lawyers during jury selection (although, unfortunately, they may occur later on).

Today, the selection of a fair jury in a case where you represent a defendant doctor is very difficult. One must attempt to understand the reasons for the difficulty, to attempt to understand some course to follow during the selection to secure the fairest possible jury.

The medical profession accuses the plaintiff's bar of the legal profession for the present so-called "crisis" in medical malpractice litigation. We know that a number of truly unmeritorious cases have been brought, and won, with substantial verdicts, by the plaintiff. But the plaintiff's malpractice bar is not so superior, nor the defendant's malpractice bar so inferior, as to permit this result. It is something more than that.

Society today does not view doctors as the respected, educated, revered, pillars of the community that it once did. The image has changed because of the patient sitting in his office until 4:00 when his appointment was at 2:00; no house calls, high bills, not being able to get him on the phone, Thursday afternoon off for golf, no Saturdays or Sundays, etc. This, of course, does not hold for the medical profession at large, but I do believe it holds for a sufficient number of members to be a significant factor in the minds of a significant number of jurors to be probably the most important element to be borne in mind when selecting the jury for a doctor.

Granted, the facts of no house calls, long waits in the office, etc., have no bearing on a doctor's professional competence, when he operates as a marketplace, in the public's mind, when he was once the esteemed savior of mankind, in the public's mind, the public will take revenge. This, coupled with the general loss of public respect for education, learning, high principles and ideals, puts the doctor in a very precarious position when he is a defendant in a lawsuit. There are jealous people who will want to "put him in his place."

How can this unfortunate situation be handled in the jury selection process?

Throughout the *voir dire,* attempt to "humanize" your client in every way that seems appropriate. Attempt to draw comparisons between the doctor's job and the job of the prospective juror you are speaking with. For example:

Q: Mr. Devine, I see from this card that they give us that you are an office administrator, is that correct?

A: Yes, sir.

Q: Just what does your job entail?

A: (At this point, the prospective juror will describe his duties, and in 99 times out of 100, you will be able to draw an analogy between his job and the doctor's job.)

Q: So, Mr. Devine, as I understand it, one of your job functions is, at the end of the day, to punch into your office computer certain statistics with respect to the day's activities in your office, for forwarding over wire to your home office, is that correct?

A: Yes, sir.

Q: Now, if you had done that, at the end of one particular day, and done it in the manner that was prescribed, and for some technical reason, over which you had no control, the information did not reach the home office due to a breakdown on the communication circuit, for example, you would not expect anyone to blame you for the material not reaching home office, would you?

A: No, I would not expect that.

Q: Similarly, Mr. Devine, if in this case you find that Dr. Best, my client, treated the plaintiff in accordance with good and accepted medical practice, but that something within the plaintiff's body, which was not within the control of Dr. Best, went wrong, and that that was the reason for the plaintiff's present physical condition, you could not fault Dr. Best for his treatment, could you?

A: No, I guess I couldn't.

Q: And, under such a circumstance, Mr. Devine, would you have any reservation at all in your mind about returning a verdict in favor of Dr. Best, even though it meant turning this unfortunate plaintiff out of court without a penny?

A: (Hopefully) No, I wouldn't.

The variations in the manner of putting this type of question are almost immeasurable, and require but the least amount of imagination. I believe that type of question to be proper, and if done often enough with enough jurors, ought to alert the jurors to the fact that the doctor is as human as they are when it comes to performing his job. The whole idea is to separate your client from the entire medical profession, so that he stands on his own two feet, and is not branded by any stigma which may attach to the medical profession at large in the juror's mind.

If this approach is utilized in the *voir dire,* and the proof in the case goes in accordance with the outline contained in the introduction to this article, very fertile ground for summation is laid.

There are certain "stock" areas of the *voir dire* in a medical malpractice case which are the same as in the *voir dire* in any civil jury case. These consist of the personal questions regarding the juror and his family, his prior jury service, his prior litigation experience, etc., and these will not be gone into here.

One is, of course, interested in the prior medical history of the juror himself, and whether he has had any untoward medical experience at all, or whether any of his close friends or members of his immediate family have had such experience. If the juror's prior medical experience causes him to criticize the doctor or hospital involved, this answer can usually be pursued by further questions, and result in either the juror evidencing a desire not to sit on this particular case because of a possible prejudice against doctors, or a legitimate challenge for cause. Conversely, in response to my question, I have been told that a juror has had a loved one die in the hospital. Having already asked the juror whether he had any untoward medical experience to himself or a member of his family, and the juror not having responded adversely to medical treatment, it is usually safe to ask him, even though the loved one died in a hospital, whether he was satisfied with the treatment. My experience indicates that in such a situation, the response will be that the juror felt that the medical body did everything they could, but still the loved one died. This of course would be a fair juror for the defendant. However, in most cases, the plaintiff will excuse this juror.

One cannot avoid what is obvious, so the defendant's lawyer must inquire, in a most general way, as to whether the jurors have read about malpractice verdicts and the malpractice situation in general in the newspapers. This must be left to the lawyer's own style and approach to the *voir dire,* and it is only he who can make a judgment by the manner of the response of the prospective juror, as well as its subject matter, whether he wants to keep the juror. Parenthetically, and it probably does not belong in an article of this type, it is most important that all lawyers should oppose any proposal that a judge select a jury for the litigants. It is, more often than not, not the response that a juror gives to a specific question, but rather the manner and demeanor of that response, which makes the decision for the lawyer. Trial lawyers must be permitted to pursue their own questioning in such areas where they have doubts as to the fairness and stability of the juror. No judge can ever do this.

In some instances, jurors indicate a reluctance to serve on a malpractice case because they are afraid it will be "too complicated." If, for one reason or another, this juror is not desired, he can usually be encouraged to talk himself off of a jury. However, if all other elements of the juror's qualifications appear adequate, and he is desired as a juror, it can usually be truthfully explained to him that the lawyers have the responsibility of presenting their proof in such a manner that the jurors understand it. Assurance can be given that that will be the case in this particular matter.

Specific inquiry should be made into the particular injury of which the plaintiff complains. The lawyer should be aware of which jurors have been exposed in one manner or another to that type of injury, and he should explore with the juror what effect, if any, it had upon him.

Although not present in the hypothetical case given in the introduction, there may be cases where the medical malpractice finding may become relevant in the *voir dire.* A general rule, which seems to make sense, is that if your client has a unanimous panel finding against him, you are duty-bound to inquire into it in the *voir dire.* The panel procedure must be explained to the prospective juror, and an effort made by whatever means at the questioner's disposal to dispel any notion that the unanimous panel finding against your client is the beginning and the end of the lawsuit. It is, of course, obvious that if litigants were prepared to accept a panel finding as binding upon all parties, they would do away with lawsuits. This, of course, has not been done. These are but two of many ways to temper the effect of a unanimous finding against your client. If there is a unanimous finding in favor of your client, it is not necessary for you to "toot" the trumpet. Rest assured that the plaintiff will, and if he does not, all the better to surprise the jurors with during the course of the trial.

If any general statement can be made as to what type of juror is most desirable for the defense in a medical malpractice case, I would have to opt for one with whom I can communicate, who is ostensibly fair, and who I believe will be able to understand the medical proofs brought forth in the case. I am aware that years ago there was effort made on the part of both the plaintiff's and the defendant's bar to select a so-called "ethnic" jury of those groups whom it was felt were predisposed to be for the plaintiff or for the defendant. It has been my experience that this largely no longer holds in any case, and, much less, a medical malpractice case. The lawyer must use his own common sense and experience in the selection of a juror with whom he feels comfortable.

It was not meant to neglect the area of jury selection on behalf of the defendant hospital in this discussion, but most of the principles applicable to representing the doctor are similarly applicable to representing the hospital, with the obvious exception of any untoward experiences any of the jurors experienced in a hospital or any experiences had by close relatives or friends. Any adverse experiences must be pursued, and, if necessary, the juror would be excused.

Obviously, this brief writing was not meant to be a comprehensive, or in-depth treatise on how to select a jury in a medical malpractice case. It was meant to convey what I consider to be certain highlights of jury selection in such a case, based upon my experience. Every lawyer has his own experiences and, of course, his own style, which must be adopted to the facts of the case with which he is confronted at any given time. Jury selection, in any case, should not be taken lightly, but this is especially so in a medical malpractice case where the injury is often horrendous, and the potential damage astronomical. Time, care, and good judgment are essential, and one who approaches the process with an attempt to fool the jurors is indeed in for a rude awakening.

CHAPTER SIXTEEN

PRESENTATION OF MEDICAL PROOF

Emmet J. Agoglia, Esq.
and
Kathleen M. Beckett, Esq.

The basic problem confronting any lawyer in a medical malpractice case is how to make a jury understand the medical concepts and issues in the case. Essentially, the lawyer must teach the jury. One does this by first teaching oneself, which develops confidence in your own ability to simplify the issues and so educate the jury to your point of view.

The key element in preparing the case lies in the selection of the issues you wish to try. Whether representing a plaintiff or defendant, the lawyer must critically analyze the case, choosing one, two or three, at most, issues which define it. The attorney for the plaintiff must, in addition to selecting the issues, try to anticipate, overcome or preclude the defenses which will be raised. This principle of issue selection is easy to enunciate, but difficult to effectuate. It requires an exhaustive knowledge and understanding of your case. While each lawyer will develop his own techniques of research and analysis, some helpful ones are set forth below.

I. CRITICAL PREPARATION

A. Definition of the Terms

Jurors, particularly in malpractice cases, are often overwhelmed by the medical terminology. Lawyers, too, are frequently pushed into a corner by their adversary's expert if they do not understand the terminology of their case. Thus, a thorough understanding of the technical terms which will be used at trial is mandatory if you are to prevail. A standard medical dictionary should be used to discover the exact definition of each word, investigating its origin or source word. For example, the word "arthroplasty" derives from the Greek "arthro," meaning joint plus "plascein," meaning to form. Once this principle of word analysis is understood by you, you can convey it to the jury, tempering their fear of such words. Moreover, the attorney gains tremendous respect from the jurors for the ease with which he handles medical terms. Respect equals a willingness to listen to the attorney which is about seventy percent of the art of advocacy. Your knowledge, in turn, will enable you to simplify the complex medical nomenclature using plain English to describe and explain each word. So, too, will your expertise enable you to prevent the opposition's medical expert witness from drowning you in his rhetoric or jargon. Having let the jury in on this secret of breaking down the terminology, it then will be better able to discern the accuracy of the statements of the witness.

The lawyer must always keep in mind Judge Holmes' wisdom: "If you let me define the terms, I shall win the argument." In short, you only try those issues you think you can win. The framing of the issues by the astute advocate requires precise definition of the terms.

B. Exhaustive Review of All Records

The lawyer must first sit down and review all medical records, be they hospital charts, doctors' office records or any other source of information, such as Workers' Compensation or Blue Cross. The source material is literally endless. When you have become totally familiar with the records, you must then review each record in detail with your medical expert. We must caution against overreliance on the ability of your expert to grasp the details of each chart. In our experience, the lawyer frequently has greater perception of the details of the case and their significance than the doctor expert. (Remember, you, the attorney, are framing the issues.) An example of this demonstrates the point: Several experts who reviewed a file overlooked the fact that a pathology report for a procedure described as removal of intestinal polyps revealed only sections of the colonic mucusa. The pathologic specimen thus clearly indicated that the operating surgeon had perforated the bowel wall rather than removing only polyps as he claimed. I'll never forget the opening address to the jury when for the first time this finding was disclosed to the defendant doctor. He actually got up and left the courtroom—never to return. Needless to say the case was settled upon the conclusion of the openings.

The hospital charts must be read again and again and again until the lawyer knows them backwards and forwards. An effective cross-examination tool is to get the defendant or his expert to go rifling through a large record looking for a significant fact. The well prepared lawyer should be able, after an appropriate delay, to instantly show the witness the precise page. This is rather easily accomplished by agreeing to number the pages of a record and reducing the critical portions to memory by number. It's amazing how you can trip a "hot shot" expert up short with such a simple device. Of course, the jury is likewise favorably impressed.

At the depositions the defendant doctor must be forced not only to read every word written on the chart, but to explain each word and the medical reasons for its use. This closes the door for novel explanations or definitions at the time of trial, thus preventing surprise.

C. Review of the Medical Literature

Preparation for trial of a malpractice case is never complete until the lawyer has reviewed the medical literature relating to the medical issues in the case. This is a time-consuming process, but well worth the effort since it gives you a working knowledge of the etiology and treatment of the condition from which your client was suffering, as well as the accepted procedures for dealing with it. Literature is also a critical element in the cross-examination of the adversary's expert witness, particularly in the Federal Court, where, unlike the State Court, you are allowed to read from it if your own expert deems it authoritative.

D. Experts

You must, whether representing a defendant or a plaintiff, spend a great deal of time with your expert, exploring the theory of your case. There must be harmony between you and the expert so that each understands the other's point of view. Don't let the physician be the lawyer! You are the expert in trial strategy—you define the goals for the trial and only you know the legal burden of proof imposed and the rules of evidence. The expert is merely one witness to help carry that burden; his testimony must fit into the overall framework of the trial or it will be of little value to your client. Another benefit of achieving harmony with your expert is in allowing the witness to be natural in responding during cross-examination, since he knows the points which must be established.

E. Preparation of Your Own Client

The accuracy of your client, whether a plaintiff or a defendant physician, is critical for the jury's acceptance of your case. Your client must accurately recall dates, conversations, symptoms, procedures performed and the like. A good method of insuring this is the use of a simple chronological guide, particularly helpful where multiple precedures have been performed over a long time span by numerous physicians. Before the trial you must decide whether you will denominate these procedures 1, 2, 3 or 4, etc., or use some other sort of descriptive phraseology. If this is not done, the jury will be lost, hopelessly bogged down in the factual details of the case, and so will never reach a point where it can focus on the issues. If you, the lawyer who has intimate knowledge of the case, cannot or will not organize it so as to highlight its critical issues, the jury surely will abandon all attempts to understand your client's viewpoint.

The same proscription is true for a defendant, particularly a physician. The witness must be able to concisely and clearly set forth the patient's history and symptoms, as well as the times they were made known to him. Where he has performed multiple procedures he too must testify accurately with respect to each procedure, giving it a simple designation, usually a numerical one, cogently setting forth the reasons for its performance. With a physician defendant, extensive preparation is necessary to insure that he is consistent in explaining the rationale behind his medical decisions. The same strictures with respect to credibility apply to a doctor defendant as to a plaintiff.

You must aim at simplicity in the presentation of your case. Therefore, laborious but necessary detail must be kept to a minimum. Some framework must be given to the jury by which facts can be expeditiously organized and retained. Here the use of charts, in multi-colors, can be of enormous value. Assume, for example, there have been four, five or six operative procedures at different times. The attorney, with the aid of a colored chart, can make this seeming maze of detail literally jump out at the jury. Such a chart might look like this:

HOSPITALIZATIONS

HOSPITAL	E.R.	ADMISSION	DISCHARGE
1. Central General	ER/ADM	9/10/81	10/25/81
2. Nassau Hospital	ADM	10/25/81	12/22/81
3. Central General	ER/ADM	12/22/81	1/19/82
4. St. Charles	RPT	1/22/82	1/22/82 (1 day)
5. Central General	ER/ADM	1/25/82	2/12/82
6. St. Charles	RPT	2/13/82	2/17/82
7. Central General	ER/ADM	2/18/82	3/27/82
8. St. Charles	RPT	4/1/82	8/11/82
9. Central General	ER/ADM	8/16/82	9/4/82
10. St. Charles	RPT/WHIRLPOOL	9/20/82	1/2/83
11. Central General	ADM	1/3/83	1/14/83
12. St. Charles	WHIRLPOOL	8/15/83	8/21/83

Your goal as a lawyer is to prevent the development of side issues—such as whether this or that procedure was preformed on a particular day—which damage your client's credibility. History and symptoms must be testified to with great accuracy, especially in a case where the malpractice involves a failure to recognize the significance of the symptoms with a consequent failure to diagnose, which prevented appropriate treatment. Some examples will serve to illustrate this point.

In a case involving a ruptured cerebral aneurysm, the history of loss of consciousness and vomiting, delirium, obtundation, photophobia, stiff neck—the cardinal signs of a bleeding aneurysm—were ignored by the treating physician, who, therefore, was unable to properly diagnose it, thus preventing timely surgical intervention so that the patient died, when, with proper treatment, he would have lived. At trial, the entire case turned on the question of the signs and symptoms presented to the attending physician. The medical experts agreed on the basic conclusions to be reached if certain signs and symptoms were present at a given time. The jury's determination turned on its belief in the accuracy of the widow's narration of symptoms, which were in sharp contrast with the defendant physician's testimony.

Another example is a rather common medical malpractice case involving a failure to diagnose acute appendicitis because the defendant physician ignored the symptoms of vomiting, nausea and fever of several days duration. His negligence resulted in the development of a severe peritonitis, which perforated the plaintiff's colon, necessitating performance of a colostomy. Once again the jury's belief in the credibility and accuracy of the plaintiff's testimony with respect to the onset and continuation of symptoms was critical to its decision.

It cannot be emphasized too strongly that your client must delineate the history and symptoms with absolute accuracy in a malpractice case. There is no leeway for uncertainty, nor ambiguity. The client must never waiver on cross-examination with respect to the history, symptoms or the medical chronology of his case. Conversely, a defendant, especially a physician, must be equally exact. A defendant's problems are slightly different, since the doctor will be aided by written notes, whether made in the office or on the hospital chart. Testimony, then, must be faithful to and consistent with such records; there can be no equivocating about what the notes did or did not mean, for the defendant, if he is to convince the jury of the merits of his position, must gain its trust in his credibility.

II. JURY SELECTION

Although this caption may, at first blush, appear to be a departure from the main topic, "Presentation of Medical Proof," nothing could be further from the fact.

The lawyer must commence the process of educating the jury during its selection. There are many ways to frame the issues by astute questioning of the jurors. For example, since medical judgment is a defense to a malpractice case, the use of the word judgment in questions to the jury puts that word and concept in their minds before they have heard a word of testimony. So, too, will questions to professional persons on the jury with respect to the standards in their profession or trade, shape the juror's thinking in terms of the issues in the case: e.g., one might ask an airline pilot if he follows a check list; a broker if he keeps up with current financial trends; a teacher or nurse if he keeps up with the current research in their respective fields. In effect, the lawyer is framing the issues during jury selection by asking these questions. The very act of framing the issues is the *sine qua non* of the presentation of medical proof.

Legal or medical terms which the jurors will hear during the course of the trial should be used in jury selection. The medical words used should graphically portray the medical issues. A simple explanation of the heart of the case should be given to the jurors in order to allow them to determine whether or not they wish to sit. The lawyer must make the prospective jurors feel comfortable and confident that they will have no difficulty understanding the medical testimony. It is far too easy for a potentially desirable juror to be frightened by his perception of the complexity of the case. Your task is to make the case comprehensible, dispelling any idea in a juror's mind that the subject matter is so complex and arcane that he will never understand it. One of the most effective ways to do this is by the technique of translating medical terms or concepts into everyday examples. Thus, a case involving a cerebral aneurysm might be likened to a leaking pipe. Once some tool is given to the jurors by which they can unravel the mysteries of medical terminology, you will find that their confidence in their ability to assess the case will be reasserted.

Naturally, the lawyers will wish to use the phraseology that the court will employ in charging the jury. So the juror should hear about departures or deviations from accepted standards of care or questions of medical judgment. Allowing the jury to become familiar with the nomenclature of the law and medicine during selection gives the attorneys more freedom in the presentation of medical proof at the later stages of the trial.

III. THE OPENING

The opening statement of the attorneys to the jury sets the tone of the case. Your success or failure will depend upon your ability to make observations which realistically relate to the testimony the jury is about to hear. The medical and legal terms must be used to skillfully frame the issues. The key to the opening statement is to keep it simple without condescension, persuasive without being argumentative. The lawyer should detail the proof that he is going to present, conveying to the jury his confidence in their ability to understand, as well as his faith in his own capacity to teach the jury everything it will need to understand about the medical proof to be offered.

To this end, the lawyer should advise the jury during the opening statement of the teaching aides which will be used during the course of the trial. Diagrams, photos, models, pathology slides and similar evidence should be utilized in explaining to the jury how your case will be proved and, more specifically, how this evidence will show that the defendant doctors departed from accepted standards of care or, alternatively, for a defendant, how they complied with such standards. For example, we have effectively used autopsy slides to conclusively demonstrate that the rupture of an aneurysm was of recent origin. This was done as part of plaintiff's prima facie proof although it also would have been used to negate the defense that the hemorrhage was of long standing and, therefore, the malpractice, if any, was in no way a proximate or contributing cause of the death. The lawyer should explain to the jury exactly how the slide will establish this fact.

So, too, must the damages be detailed to the jury with an explanation of the manner in which the damages are related to the departure of the defendants. Thus, where the plaintiff has suffered from peritonitis as a result of the failure to diagnose an appendicitis, the opening statement must describe the progression from appendicitis to peritonitis to colostomy performed following rupture of the colon due to the infection. Subsequent surgeries and medical care must be related to the initial failure to diagnose. Then any other damages flowing from the negligence of the defendants should be outlined.

The opening statement should provide the order of proof, as well as prepare the jury for the witnesses who will be called, the reasons they are being called and what you expect to prove from each witness. This will help prevent the jury from being sidetracked into peripheral issues.

Any questions with respect to the contributory negligence of your client should be addressed in the opening, which should make clear to the jury that the very reason for the plaintiff coming under the medical care and treatment of the defendants was that he sustained some prior injury or illness. Almost every malpractice case, of necessity, involves a sick or hurt plaintiff before the treatment even starts. If the jury clearly understands this, the plaintiff can take away defendant's arguments about contributory negligence. An example was given in the case of a jogger who collapsed from heatstroke. By making certain the jury understood it was his collapse which delivered him to the hands of the defendant physicians, the issue of whether or not he should be jogging, which defendants tried to raise, was removed from the case. In other words, the jury must be made to recognize that the negligence starts with the medical treatment, not with the events which took place before the jogger was brought to the emergency room. If the opening statement does not clearly delineate such an issue, you will find the jury lost in a morass of facts which will prevent them from being able to follow the testimony intelligently. An orderly, simple and informative opening statement will give your client a great advantage in the case.

IV. ORDER OF PROOF (OR ORDER OF WITNESSES)

One of the most challenging facets of presenting the medical proof is the order of witnesses. The order in which witnesses are presented to the jury is a crucial factor in any case, but one frequently overlooked by lawyers. Many times in a medical malpractice case it is wise for the plaintiff to put the defendant physician on as the first witness. This allows the jury to form its own impression of the defendant before it is jaded by other testimony. The use of the defendant physician as plaintiff's first witness is particularly effective if the advocate feels he has some excellent material to impune the credibility of the defendant. We all know that jurors are most critical of the early witnesses, especially jurors who have never sat previously. The order in which your expert witness or witnesses are presented must be given a great deal of thought. Do you wish to use them early in the case to set forth the standards of care and the departures therefrom, or do you prefer to finish up your case with such witnesses so that the last testimony before the jury is of your expert. This critical atmosphere dissipates as the testimony piles up. The jurors almost get accustomed to inconsistency or even contradictions.

Calling the defendant first also prevents the defense from preparing the witness on a day to day basis as proof goes on. Each case must be decided on its own peculiar facts. Since malpractice cases are traditionally full trials (i.e., the liability and damages litigated at one time), the damage witnesses must be woven into the fabric of your case. There is no set format. You must decide the order of proof which is most advantageous to the particular case. In making this decision do not forget that documentary proof, too, gains or loses impact from the timing of its introduction, so that it must also be considered as another witness in the order of proof.

V. DEMONSTRATIVE EVIDENCE

We have deliberately intertwined throughout this text the concept of demonstrative evidence but have saved it for the end of the chapter.

Refer again to the above chart showing the various hospital stays of the plaintiff. Now imagine that you have skillfully prepared the exhibit so that no proper objection can be proffered to its offer. Allow it to sit in front of a jury on a stand for two or three days. Every time the jury is bored (and it's going to happen in any and every trial), it can turn to the exhibit and appreciate the extent of the disability and suffering of the plaintiff. Now join with that exhibit another which charts each admission diagnosis, the surgery performed during the hospital stay and the discharge diagnosis. Parenthetically do we point out that this chart must also be introduced with great care and caution and after all proper foundations have been established. As your treating physician expert testifies he has before him a visible ready reference that makes for a smooth flow of what could be otherwise laborious testimony. As a rule of thumb we would suggest that if you're having difficulty with the sequence of treatment, the jury will likewise be similarly perplexed and in those instances a chart or other such device must be used. The reason for its use is to make real the horror of the wrong done to the client.

The use of enlarged X-rays (again only after a proper foundation is established) can be most effective. We like to ask the court to turn out or at least dim the room lights so that all attention is focused on a critical X-ray. You don't want the jury distracted by the antics of your adversary or anyone else at this juncture. The movie-like atmosphere can insure that there will be no untoward interruptions.

Medical models, be they plastic, or better still real skeletons, are another useful tool in the presentation of medical proof. For example, when the issue is the misdiagnosis of an ankle fracture, it is imperative that a jury see an ankle joint so that the verbal description can be polished by visual demonstration. Presentation of medical proof is no different than any other teaching technique. The more senses one can involve, the easier the learning experience.

When the issue is the claim of neglect during a complex surgical procedure, the defense can effectively demonstrate the difficulty of working in such an obstructed area. Detailed drawings, such as the "F. Netter" variety found in all good medical texts, dramatically display the lack of vision, etc., with which the surgeon is working. The opposition must be prepared to establish that an inadvertent puncture of the urethra could be understandable, but the failure to dye test before closure is a departure from good and accepted surgical practice.

In conclusion, the methods of presentation of demonstrative evidence are limited only by the imagination of the advocate. We, for example, have not even alluded to the use of motion pictures because their use is so widely discussed in most trial practice seminars. But the devices we are suggesting have a limited cost factor and can be used in all types of medical malpractice claims, be they major or minor cases.

VI. SUMMATION

Where the case has been properly presented, the summation will virtually deliver itself. Nonetheless, the astute attorney will concentrate his summation of the key issue of the case, weaving together the strands of evidence so as to emphasize to the jury how the proof supports his case. Where there has been testimony which tends to obfuscate and to confuse, the must show the jury its irrevelance to the issues at bar. He might also point out that such testimony is designed to confuse, indicating to them his confidence in their intellectual capacity to perceive this ruse. An effective summation will integrate liability and damages, putting before the jury a coherent picture of the case. If you, the lawyer, have successfully presented the proof, then the court's charge will flow naturally from your last words to the jury.

CHAPTER SEVENTEEN

THE DEFENDANT PHYSICIAN AS PLAINTIFF'S WITNESS

Stanley A. Landers, Esq.

I. INTRODUCTION

There are several good reasons for the plaintiff to subpoena the defendant physician as his witness in a medical malpractice case. For plaintiff to call the defendant to the stand on his case, especially as the first witness, usually proves to be effective drama in the courtroom. It also takes the wind out of the sails of one of the defense's best witnesses and frequently leaves defense counsel on the horns of a real dilemma: whether to immediately ''cross-examine'' his own witness to restore credibility or to postpone any questioning until the defendant's part of the case. Pragmatically, it may help plaintiff's counsel in the scheduling of his other witnesses. Sometimes plaintiff may even be able to make out a prima facie case using the defendant physician as his own expert.

Once the decision has been made to call the defendant physician as part of plaintiff's case, experience has shown that to insure successful questioning a brief memorandum of law should be given to the court beforehand. A memorandum is presented on the next page.

After the trial judge has been educated about your plan and its sound legal basis, intensive preparation for the questioning must be done. Unlike the other witnesses who will testify for plaintiff, to whom open-ended questions should frequently be asked, the questioning of the defendant, obviously a hostile witness, is really in the nature of cross-examination and must be very tight.

The old adage that a lawyer should not ask a question in court to which he does not know the answer has greatest application when questioning the defendant. The key ingredient to success in this regard is obviously a good examination before trial. In fact, the questioning can easily be turned into virtual ''testimony'' by the plaintiff's attorney himself, by simply taking the statement gleaned from the deposition, and then adding, ''Is that correct, Doctor?'' This is illustrated in the sample questioning below.

Finally, the problem will often arise that the defendant (or the expert who the defendant will later call) will seek to wiggle out of the legal straitjacket in which you seek to place him by giving long-winded, complicated medical explanations. This must not be permitted! Do not attempt to fight on his battlefield. As soon as this occurs, very politely ask the physician if he would enter into an agreement with you: Would he please answer your questions with either a "yes" or "no," or, if he cannot do so, say so and you will ask another question. Most trial judges will allow this if done early and in a respectful manner.

A short sample is finally presented to illustrate the principles discussed.

II. SAMPLE QUESTIONING OF THE DEFENDANT PHYSICIAN AS PLAINTIFF'S WITNESS

(The claim was that placental fragments left in the uterus after delivery caused hemorrhaging eight days later requiring a hysterectomy. The defense claimed the hysterectomy was inevitable bacause of a condition known as focal placenta accreta, wherein one part of the placenta penetrates the lining of the uterus.)

Q: You are a physician licensed to practice medicine in the State of New York?

A: Yes.

Q: You have limited your practice of medicine to the specialty of obstetrics and gynecology for the last 20 years?

A: Yes.

Q: After seeing the plaintiff, Mrs. P., at your office for eight prenatal checkups, you had her admitted to the defendant hospital, through your service, on January 1, 1982, is that correct?

A: Yes.

Q: And at approximately 9:00 a.m. you delivered a live baby girl?

A: Yes.

Q. Now, Doctor, physicians speak of the birth of a child as taking place in three stages, is that correct?

A: Yes.

Q: And the third stage, which occurs after the child is born, involves the delivery of the placenta, which is also known as the afterbirth, correct?

A: Yes.

Q: Do you agree with me, Doctor, that it is good practice for a physician to carefully inspect the placenta after delivery to see that none of it is missing and may have been left behind in the uterus?

A: Yes.

Q: And conversely, if a physician fails to inspect the placenta carefully after delivery, that constitutes a departure from good medical practice, isn't that so, Doctor?

A: I would have to say yes.

Q: Now Doctor, when Mrs. P. was readmitted to the hospital on January 9, 1982, and underwent a dilation and curettage, or D&C, as well as a subsequent hysterectomy, the pathology report of the specimens submitted showed "a large amount of placental tissue," is that correct?

A: Well, that was because of the plaintiff's unusual condition of focal placenta accreta. It was inevitable. Part of her placenta had penetrated through the uterine wall.

Q: Doctor, in an effort to move the questioning along, could we enter into an agreement? Would you try to simply answer my next few questions with a "yes" or "no," or if you cannot do so, tell me and I will ask another question? Will you try to do that?

A: If I can.

Q: Thank you. Doctor, did the pathologist, the specialist in making both gross and microscopic analyses of tissue, in both parts of his report describe his findings as "a large amount of placental tissue?"

A: Yes.

Q: And that same report indicates that 30 c.c.s of such tissue was found?

A: Yes.

Q: And Doctor, 30 cubic centimeters is the same as 30 milliliters, such as is marked off on this flask, correct?

A: Yes.

(Flask offered into evidence)

Q: Doctor, if you carefully examined a placenta after its delivery you would notice it if 30 c.c.s were missing, correct?

A: Possibly.

Q: (Looking at jury) But if you don't look at something you can never see it, correct Doctor?

OBJECTION!

TRIAL MEMORANDUM

It is beyond question that when plaintiff calls defendant as a witness he may (1) cross-examine him, which includes the right to ask leading questions and not be bound by the answers; and (2) question him as a medical expert.

In the case of *Segreti v. Putnam Community Hospital*, 88 A.D.2d 590 (1982), the Court stated: ''The trial court also erred in improperly curtailing plaintiff's examination of defendant Chang as a hostile and an expert witness. As an adverse party, Dr. Chang was a hostile witness subject to cross-examination when called to the stand by plaintiff.'' *Gonzalez v. Medina*, 69 A.D.2d 14.

The famous Court of Appeals case of *Becker v. Koch*, 104 N.Y. 394, is frequently cited for the same proposition. *See also Richardson on Evidence*, 10th Edition, Section 483, page 472.

The Court in *Segreti* further opined: ''It is well-settled law that a plaintiff in a medical malpractice action may call as a witness the doctor against whom she brought the action and question him as a medical expert.'' *See McDermott v. Manhattan Eye, Ear and Throat Hosp.*, 15 N.Y.2d 20. It was further emphasized that this principle applies even where plaintiff ''was able to employ other expert witnesses besides Dr. Chang'' (the defendant).

Respectfully submitted,

Attorney for Plaintiff

CHAPTER EIGHTEEN

EXPERT OPINION IN MEDICAL MALPRACTICE CASES

Thomas J. Principe, Esq.

In this paper I will discuss three divisions of the law regarding the use of expert testimony in medical malpractice cases: (I) the necessity of expert testimony, (II) the qualifications of the expert witness, (III) the nature of the expert testimony.

I. THE NECESSITY OF EXPERT TESTIMONY

Although occasionally the doctrine of *res ipsa loquitur* may be a substitute for expert testimony, such testimony in a medical malpractice case is a practical necessity and virtually a legal requirement. Unless the matter on which testimony is sought is within the comprehension of laymen and requires only common knowledge and experience to understand, expert evidence on the issue of negligence is essential to support an action for malpractice against a physician or surgeon.[1]

To qualify as an expert, the witness must have acquired special knowledge of the subject matter about which he is to testify.[2] The determination of the competency and qualifications of a medical witness is made by the trial judge in his discretion and his ruling will not be disturbed by a reviewing court unless the trial judge has abused his discretion or his error is clear and involves a misconception of the law.[3]

A. The Legal Necessity

Some New York courts have held unequivocally that expert medical testimony is required to establish even a *prima facie* case of malpractice. Only when the very nature of acts complained of bespeaks improper treatment and malpractice is there no requirement to substantiate the impropriety of such acts by expert medical testimony.[4]

For example, in *Hale v. State of New York*, decided in 1976,[5] the Appellate Division, Fourth Department held that in most instances in a medical malpractice case, expert testimony must be presented to make out a *prima facie* case. More pertinently, in *Heggar v. Green*,[6] the Second Circuit, interpreting New York law, held that the plaintiff in a medical malpractice action has the burden to produce expert testimony.

B. The Practical Necessity

These decisions may state the rule in terms that are too absolute. Nevertheless, the use of expert testimony is a practical requirement even if it is not a literal requirement. Thus in *Toth v. Community Hospital at Glen Cove*,[7] the New York Court of Appeals held that in a medical malpractice case, a patient does not always require expert testimony to establish a *prima facie* case. In *Koehler v. Schwartz*,[8] however, the court made it clear that the extent to which a sharp curette might contribute to success of an abortion was not a matter of common knowledge which a jury could determine in the absence of expert testimony. Therefore, the plaintiff's attorney should operate on the assumption that he will need to offer expert testimony.[9]

C. *Res Ipsa Loquitur*

Of course, a medical expert is not always available. Frequently, a plaintiff, because of his inability to obtain a proper expert, will attempt to use the doctrine of *res ipsa loquitur* to establish his *prima facie* case. This doctrine may be used in medical malpractice cases in the absence of expert testimony. *Res ipsa loquitur* is also applicable when an expert testifies that the medical events and the resulting injury would not have occurred without some act of negligence.[10]

For example, in *Derrell v. Nassau County Medical Center*,[11] the plaintiff relied on the doctrine of *res ipsa loquitur* to establish the defendant hospital's negligence. In that case, an infant had its leg in a cast, and while the infant lay on a stretcher, the stretcher collapsed. The evidence showed that after the accident one of the stretcher's wheels was found on the ground. Although no one actually saw the stretcher fall, the nurse testified that the infant could not have moved the stretcher herself. Therefore, the Appellate Division, Second Department found that the inference of defendant's negligence and the plaintiff's freedom from contributory negligence made the application of *res ipsa loquitur* inescapable. Additionally in *Prooth v. Walsh*,[12] the doctrine of *res ipsa loquitur* was utilized where a surgical clamp was inadvertently left in a plaintiff's chest cavity during a heart bypass operation.

Some trial courts, however, do not always find the doctrine applicable. In *DeFalco v. Long Island College Hospital*,[13] the court rejected the plaintiff's contention that a drop of blood found in his eye after a cataract operation was an appropriate occasion for the application of the doctrine. The court also held that the presence of an infection which appeared after the surgery did not automatically give rise to an inference of negligence on the part of the surgeon or hospital. Thus, expert testimony was necessary.

D. The Uses of Expert Testimony

Parties actually usc cxpert testimony in two different situations.

In *Dougherty v. Milliken*,[14] a case in which expert testimony was offered to show negligence in the construction of a derrick, the New York Court of Appeals distinguished the two situations:

> It may be broadly stated as a general proposition that there are two classes of cases in which expert testimony is admissible. To the one class belong those cases in which the conclusions to be drawn by the jury depend upon the existence of facts which are not common knowledge and which are peculiarly within the knowledge of men whose experience or study enables them to speak with authority upon the subject. If, in such cases, the jury with all the facts before them can form a conclusion thereon, it is their sole province to do so. In the other class we find those cases in which the conclusions to be drawn from the facts stated, as well as knowledge, of the facts themselves, depend upon professional or scientific knowledge or skill not within the range of ordinary training or intelligence. In such cases not only the facts, but the conclusions to which they lead, may be testified to by qualified experts.

In either situation, a party's offer to introduce expert testimony raises three questions regarding the admissibility of the testimony.

E. The Admissibility of Expert Testimony

New York's rule on the admissibility of expert testimony originated in the venerable case of *Jones v. Tucker*,[15] which held that the admission of expert opinion is grounded in necessity. In *Jones v. Tucker*, the court held that three questions arise when a party offers expert testimony:

1. Can the opinion of an expert be received on the subject?
2. What are the qualifications which entitle a witness to testify as an expert?
3. Does the witness have those qualifications?

The trial court must answer all of these questions in the affirmative before the expert testimony will be admitted: the question is appropriate, particular qualifications are ascertainable, and the witness possesses those qualifications.

II. THE QUALIFICATIONS OF THE EXPERT WITNESS

Since we have established the appropriateness, indeed the necessity, of expert medical testimony, let us discuss the necessary qualifications of the witness, a couple of particular specialties, and the stricter rule in other states as compared with New York.

A. The Expert Witness Need Not be a Specialist

According to most courts, a physician or surgeon is not incompetent to testify as an expert merely because he is not a specialist in the particular branch of his profession involved in the case. An example is *Fuller v. Pries*,[16] in which the New York Court of Appeals held that a physician licensed to practice medicine may be qualified as an expert in any branch of medicine, despite the fact that he was not a specialist in that branch. In *Fuller*[17] the neurologist who did not practice psychiatry testified as a medical expert concerning decedent's lack of control over his conduct in an action to recover for the suicide of the decedent. The fact that he was not a specialist should only go the weight to be given to the testimony and not its admissibility. Also, in *Carbone v. Warburton*,[18] which involved a medical malpractice action against a specialist, an 82-year-old physician who had been retired for twenty years, who was licensed in another state, and who was not a specialist in the field to which the action related, was held competent to testify as an expert. Additionally, in *Meiselman v. Crown Heights Hospital*,[19] the New York Court of Appeals held that it was error not to permit a surgeon educated and trained in foreign countries to testify as an expert on the ground that he was not competent to testify as to the proper practice in America in 1932, since he was not admitted to practice in this country until 1936.

Morever, physicians in general practice are generally competent to give opinions regarding injuries to, or the proper treatment for, diseases or injuries to the body.[20] In *People v. Benham*,[21] the New York Court of Appeals held that a physician who had read the applicable medical authorities before reaching his conclusion could testify concerning the effects of prussic acid, although he was a practicing physician and not a toxicologist.

There are other examples from other courts. In *Frost v. Mayo Clinic*,[22] plaintiff sued alleging a failure to do a neurosurgical decompression of a spinal disc. The United States District Court, Third Division, Minnesota, held that the testimony of a qualified medical doctor could not be excluded simply because he was not a neurosurgeon. The court was of the opinion that the matter of training and specialization of the witness goes to the weight rather than the admissibility of the testimony. A further example is seen in *Fitzmaurice v. Flynn*,[23] wherein a malpractice action was brought against an obstetrician-gynecologist for failure to properly diagnose and determine the nature of a lump in a patient's breast. The Supreme Court of Connecticut held it to be reversible error to refuse to allow expert testimony by a surgeon specializing in breast cancer surgery on the ground that his expertise was in another field and that he thus lacked competency to testify. The Connecticut Court stated that it is the scope of the witness' knowledge and not the artificial classification by title that should govern the threshold question of admissibility.

However, there have been other cases in which the courts have been more selective when deciding whether a physician could testify as an expert. Let us consider two examples: podiatry and chiropractic.

B. Two Apparent Exceptions

When dealing with malpractice on the part of podiatrists, the courts have been divided as to whether a physician can testify as a medical witness.

In *Darby v. Cohen*,[24] the trial court, citing the Appellate Division, Second Department, case of *Taormina v. Goodman*,[25] held that a physician could not render expert opinion as to the standard of care and departure therefrom by a podiatrist, since medicine and podiatry are two separate forms of health care and podiatry is not a branch of medicine. In *Darby*, plaintiff's expert, who was not allowed to testify at trial, was a general surgeon. The trial court referred to *People v. D. Scholl's Foot Comfort Shops*,[26] in which the New York Court of Appeals made the distinction between podiatry and medicine and held that while dentistry is a branch of medicine, podiatry is not.

The same reasoning was used in *Whitehurst v. Boehm*,[27] where the North Carolina Court of Appeals held that the standard of care required of a podiatrist cannot be established through testimony of an orthopedic surgeon. It can only be established by testimony of another podiatrist or someone equally familiar with the field of practice. However, in *Goldstein v. Madison Avenue Hospital*,[28] the trial court held that it was not error to allow a medical doctor to testify as an expert witness on podiatric practice, inasmuch as the defendant had been acting as a surgeon when the negligent act took place.

When we turn to our second example, chiropractic, we find that the courts have long held that a chiropractor is competent to testify as an expert or medical witness concerning matters within the scope of the profession and practice of a chiropractic.[29] Moreover, when the proper foundation has been laid and the matter is within the scope of the profession and practice of chiropractic, a chiropractor is also competent to express his opinion as to the nature and extent of injuries to portions of the human body to which the chiropractic segment of medical science relates. However, since chiropractic is a form of health care separate and distinct from the practice of medicine, the courts have been reluctant to allow physicians to testify as to the standard of care for chiropractors. For instance, in *Taormina v. Goodman*,[30] the Appellate Division, Second Department, reversed a finding for the plaintiff where the testimony of a physician was used to establish a deviation from the standard of care by a chiropractor. The court specifically held that chiropractic is separate and distinct from the practice of medicine. The court went on to say that where a chirpractor departs from the restrictions placed upon the practice of his profession, *see* Education Law, sec. 6551, and ventures into the practice of medicine, then a physician's standards would apply. In *Vidra v. Shoman*,[31] another Second Department case, the court made it clear that chiropractors do not practice medicine and would thus not be qualified to testify against, say, an orthopedist in the area of departure from good and accepted medical practice.

A similar finding was made in *Maxwell v. McCaffrey*,[32] where the Supreme Court of Virginia held that the plaintiff could not introduce the testimony of an orthopedic surgeon as an expert against a chiropractor, on the grounds that the surgeon was not familiar with the standards of skill and care exercised by chiropractors in Virginia.

In summary, we can conclude that physicians are generally qualified to testify as experts on medical aspects of personal injuries. However, courts in some states do require a physician to possess more specific and relevant qualifications before allowing him to testify as an expert. Thus, those courts have held that in order to qualify as an expert, a medical witness must have some familiarity with the particular medical or surgical technique involved in the suit, unless the technique is so unusual that the defendant is its sole practitioner.[33]

C. Familiarity With The Technique

Given the necessity that the witness be familiar with the particular technique, what type of familiarity will be sufficient for the witness to qualify as an expert? Some courts speak of actual or practical knowledge (often termed "occupational experience"), of how a physician or surgeon uses the technique involved and have held the view that the witness must have used the technique himself.[34] Other courts have held that while some familiarity with the technique is necessary, the witness may have acquired that familiarity by other means, such as private study, observation or consultation with other physicians and surgeons.[35] This stricter rule seems to be more sensible in an age of medical specialization, but New York has not adopted it.

III. THE NATURE OF THE EXPERT'S TESTIMONY

Once a party has established that his witness is qualified to testify as an expert, the expert must testify on the basis of a sound hypothesis, but he need not testify to a medical certainty. An expert will be called to render an opinion of the relevant standard of care and on the issue of causation.

A. A Sound Hypothesis

The expert's opinion must be based on a sound hypothesis or the opinion lacks probative force. In *Quinones v. St. Vincent's Hospital*,[36] plaintiff's expert testified that plaintiff sustained traumatic fractures of cervical vertebrae in her neck in the period during which she was undergoing an unrelated operation or while she was recovering from the effects of the anesthetic given to her during that operation. The Appellate Division, First Department, held that hospital records, the X-rays of plaintiff's neck, and the testimony of the attending doctor provided a satisfactory explanation for the plaintiff's cervical injuries, namely that they were the result of an infection and not due to trauma. The First Department held that a finding that the plaintiff had sustained traumatic injury during the time of the operation, or the period of unconsciousness thereafter, would rest upon mere surmise or speculation.

B. Medical Certainty Unnecessary

However, expert opinion does not need to rest on a degree of medical certainty to be admissible. In *Matott v. Ward*,[37] the New York Court of Appeals held that the opinion of an expert need reflect only a degree of confidence sufficient to satisfy accepted standards of reliability. The *Matott* case involved a collision between a car driven by the plaintiff and the defendant's van. The court asked the plaintiff's treating physician whether he could say with a degree of medical certainty that the plaintiff's present condition was caused solely by the accident without any other accident intervening. The physician replied that he did not think he could say with certainty that the plaintiff's condition at the time of trial was due solely to the accident. The witness subsequently volunteered that he had mistakenly assumed that the judge's earlier inquiry demanded absolute certainty, and he then proceeded to answer in the affirmative.

Judge Fuchsberg, writing for a unanimous court, characterized the phrase "with a reasonable degree of medical certainty," as a "single verbal straight jacket." Thus, so long as the opinion is not based on a guess or a surmise, and gives the assurance of satisfying a standard of reliability, it will have probative force and be deemed sufficient to allow the issue to go to the jury.

An even more recent example decided in January 1983, is *Lipsius v. White*.[38] In that case the Appellate Division, Second Department, reversed the trial court which had dismissed the complaint at the close of the evidence. The Appellate Court held that the testimony of the patient's medical expert regarding an operation upon the patient's right hand raised the issue of unnecessary surgery and lack of informed consent which should have been submitted to a jury. There was sufficient evidence to support a finding that the physician had deviated from the accepted standards of medical practice by failing to perform certain preoperative diagnostic tests and thereby, to comprehend the true nature of the symptoms presented, and that such departure "proximately caused the undertaking of an operation which should never have been recommended or undertaken."[39] The court cited the 1964 New York

Court of Appeals decision in *McDermott v. Manhattan Eye, Ear and Throat Hospital.*[40]

In other words, testimony of medical certainty is not necessary to raise a question of fact for the jury.

IV. CONCLUSION

This has been a brief overview of three aspects of the use of expert testimony in medical malpractice cases: the necessity of such testimony, the qualifications of the witness, and the nature of the testimony.

I have not undertaken in this paper to deal with particular problems of proof for particular injuries. However, I hope I have led you to further fruitful research on these three aspects of expert testimony.

Footnotes

[1] 81 ALR 2d 597; *Dougherty v. Milliken*, 163 N.Y. 527 (1900); *Meiselman v. Crown Heights Hospital*, 285 N.Y. 389, 34 N.E.2d 367 (1941).

[2] 31 Am. Jur. 2d secs. 26 and 27; *Richardson on Evidence*, 10th ed., sec. 367. Pegalis & Wachsman, *American Law of Medical Malpractice*, Vol. 2, sec. 11.1.

[3] 31 Am. Jur. 2d sec. 31; *Slocovich v. Orient Mutual Ins Co.*, 108 N.Y. 56, 14 N.E. 82 (1888); *Inland and Seaboard Coasting Co. v. Tolson*, 139 U.S. 551, 77 S. Ct. 653, 35 L. Ed. 270 (1983).

[4] *Morgan v. State of New York*, 40 A.D.2d 891, 337 N.Y.S.2d 536 (3d Dep't, 1972), *appeal denied*, 31 N.Y.2d 974, 341 N.Y.S.2d 310, 293 N.E.2d 558 (1973).

[5] 53 A.D.2d 1025, 386 N.Y.S.2d 151 (4th Dep't, 1976).

[6] 646 F.2d 22 (2d Cir. 1981).

[7] 22 N.Y.2d 255, 292 N.Y.S.2d 440 (1968).

[8] 48 N.Y.2d 807, 424 N.Y.S.2d 119 (1979).

[9] The legislature recently amended CPLR 3101. A party must now disclose, before the trial, the identity and the qualification of each witness, the subject matter and the substance of his testimony, and the grounds for his opinion. However, in an action for medical malpractice, a party may decline to disclose the names of his medical experts. It appears that after having recognized both the need and to a large extent the solution in dealing with the mysteries surrounding experts in medical malpractice cases, the legislature decided, for no explainable reason, that the names of experts may be omitted in cases of medical or dental malpractice. How a party can disclose an expert's qualifications without indirectly disclosing his identity remains to be seen.

[10] *Richardson on Evidence*, *supra*, 10th ed, sec. 93.

[11] 73 A.D.2d 682, 423 N.Y.S.2d 845 (2d Dep't, 1979).

[12] 105 Misc. 2d 603, 432 N.Y.S.2d 663 (1980).

[13] 90 Misc. 2d 164, 432 N.Y.S.2d 663, *aff'd,* 62 A.D.2d 1180 (2d Dep't, 1977).

[14] 163 N.Y. 527, 57 N.E. 757 (1900).

[15] 41 N.H. 546 (1860).

[16] 35 N.Y.2d 425, 363 N.Y.S.2d 568, 322 N.E.2d 263 (1974).

[17] *Fuller v. Pries*, 363 N.Y.2d at 575; *see also People v. Rice*, 159 N.Y. 400, 54 N.E. 48 (1900).

[18] 22 N.J. Super 5, 91 A.2d 518 (1952).

[19] *Meiselman v. Crown Heights Hospital*, 285 N.Y. at 398-399.

[20] *Pridgen v. Gibson*, 194 N.C. 289, 139 S.E. 443 (1927); *Cooper v. St. Paul City*, 54 Minn. 379, 56 N.W. 42 (1893).

[21] 160 N.Y. 402, 55 N.E. 11 (1899).

[22] 304 F. Supp 285 (DC Minn., 1969).

[23] 167 Conn. 609, 356 A.2d 881 (1975).

[24] 101 Misc. 2d 516, 421 N.Y.S.2d 337 (1979).

[25] 63 A.D.2d 1018, 406 N.Y.S.2d 350 (2d Dep't, 1978).

[26] 277 N.Y. 151, 13 N.E.2d 750 (1938).

[27] 41 N.C. App. 670, 255 S.E.2d 761 (1979).

[28] N.Y.L.J. August 27, 1981, p. 12, col. 4.

[29] *Johnston v. Peairs*, 117 Cal. App. 208, 3 P.2d 617 (1931); *Voight v. Industrial Com.*, 297 Ill. 109, 130 N.E. 470 (1921); O'Dell v. Barrett, 163 Md. 342, 163 A. 191 (1932).

[30] *Taormina v. Goodman*, 63 A.D.2d at 1017 (1978).

[31] 59 A.D.2d 714, 398 N.Y.S.2d 377 (2d Dep't, 1977).

[32] 219 Va. 909, 252 S.E.2d 342 (1979).

[33] *See* annotations at 141 ALR 5; 81 ALR 2d 597.

[34] *Pearce v. Linde*, 113 Cal. App. 2d 627, 248 P.2d 506 (1952); *Sevanson v. Chatterton*, 281 Minn. 129, 160 N.W.2d 662 (1968).

[35] *Bisendine v. Hunt*, 43 Ga. App. 115, 158 S.E. 469 (1931); *McCoy v. Beeck*, 87 Ind. App. 3, 157 N.E. 456 (1927); *Carbone, supra*.

[36] 20 A.D.2d 529, 244 N.Y.S.2d 690 (1st Dep't, 1963), *aff'd*, 16 N.Y.2d 572, 260 N.Y.S.2d 842.

[37] 48 N.Y.2d 455, 423 N.Y.S.2d 645, 399 N.E.2d 532 (1979).

[38] 91 A.D.2d 271, 458 N.Y.S.2d 928 (2d Dep't, 1983).

[39] *Ibid*, at 933.

[40] 15 N.Y.2d 20, 255 N.Y.S.2d 65, 203 N.E.2d 469 (1964).

CHAPTER NINETEEN

THE USE OF MEDICAL TREATISES AND TEXTS

Ira A. Cohen, Esq.

Medical experts in malpractice cases have a natural advantage over their attorney interrogator during cross-examinations; for although the trial occurs upon the lawyer's physical battlefield, the intellectual battlefield usually belongs to the expert. In the minds of the jurors, the doctor begins the examination with an aura of expertise, and it is the attorney's duty to break through the mystique and show the jurors that the expert's opinion is suspect.

I. OPINIONS HELD BY MEDICAL EXPERTS

Because an expert's testimony is based upon both his experience and his learning, "it is perfectly proper to ask him whether or not the opinion he has expressed agrees with the opinion of other people who are conceded to be learned upon the same subject." *Egan v. Dry Dock, E.B. & B.R. Co.*, 42 N.Y.S. 188, 12 A.D. 556 (1st Dep't, 1896). If the rule "were otherwise, men of insufficient learning or veritable quacks, might palm off their crude opinions on juries as scientific knowledge." *Brownell and Wife v. Black*, 31 N.Br. 594.

II. ADVANTAGES OF USING MEDICAL LITERATURE DURING CROSS-EXAMINATION

The ability to cross-examine the medical expert by confronting him with the relevant, authoritative medical literature is an important weapon in the cross-examiner's arsenal, and one which aids in equalizing the intellectual battle between expert and attorney. First, jurors tend to believe the written word, and showing that an expert's opinion differs materially from opinions expressed in learned and authoritative books and articles goes far in shaking jurors' confidence in the infallibility of the expert's opinion. Second, an expert denying familiarity with certain published works may cause jurors to believe that he is behind the times. Finally, an expert refusing to acknowledge the authoritativeness of certain books and treatises will appear to the jurors to be evasive, uncooperative and inflexible.

III. VARIATIONS AMONG JURISDICTIONS

While all jurisdictions to some extent allow the cross-examination of experts by reading from authoritative sources in contradiction of the witness' opinion, the specific rules governing such use of treatises differ among the various courts. Some states require that the expert witness must have relied upon the particular treatise on direct examination before he can be cross-examined on the same treatise. Other states also require reliance upon the specific treatise, but allow the fact to be established during cross-examination. More liberal states have dispensed with the reliance requirement, but require that the witness recognize the work as authoritative before he can be cross-examined through the use of opinions expressed in the treatise. Finally, the most liberal jurisdictions allow the use of the treatise on cross-examination so long as its status as an authority is established by any means.

IV. THE NEW YORK RULE

The rule in New York is that a medical expert (including a defendant doctor) may be confronted on cross-examination with a passage from a treatise which the expert recognizes as authoritative and which is contrary to his testimony. *Egan v. Dry Dock, supra*; *Ciaccio v. Housman*, 411 N.Y.S.2d 524, 97 Misc. 2d 367 (1978); *Hastings v. Chrysler Corp.*, 77 N.Y.S.2d 524, 273 A.D. 292 (1st Dep't, 1948); *Mark v. Colgate University*, 395 N.Y.S.2d 621, 53 A.D.2d 884 (2nd Dep't, 1976). The expert does not have to have read the book, or relied upon it in his own testimony, but he must have acknowledged its authoritativeness. *Hastings v. Chrysler Corp.*, *supra*; *Mark v. Colgate University*, *supra*. Such treatises can be used for impeachment purposes only, and may not be offered as evidence in chief or as substantive affirmative evidence of the facts or opinions contained therein. *Egan v. Dry Dock*, *supra*; *Foggett v. Fischer*, 48 N.Y.S. 741, 23 A.D. 207 (2nd Dep't, 1897); *Phillips v. Roux Laboratories*, 145 N.Y.S.2d 449, 286 A.D. 549 (1st Dep't, 1955); *Ciaccio v. Houseman*, *supra*; *Rosario v. New York City Health & Hospitals Corp.*, 450 N.Y.S.2d 805, 87 A.D.2d 211 (1st Dep't, 1982); *Cummings v. Fondale*, 474 N.Y.S.2d 356, 122 Misc. 2d 913 (App. Term. 1st Dep't, 1983).

V. THE FEDERAL RULE

The Federal rule governing learned treatises is more liberal than New York's rule, and affords the cross-examiner considerably more leeway. Federal Rule of Evidence 803(18) states that the following is an exception to the hearsay rule:

> (18)Learned Treatises. To the extent called to the attention of an expert witness upon cross-examination or relied upon by him in direct examina-

tion, statements contained in published treatises, periodicals, or pamphlets on a subject of history, medicine or other science or art, established as a reliable authority by the testimony or admission of the witness or by other expert testimony or by judicial notice. If admitted the statements may be read into evidence but may not be received as exhibits.

Rule 803(18) does not require that the expert rely upon or recognize the treatise as authoritative, thus avoiding the possibility that he may at the outset block cross-examination by refusing to concede reliance or authoritativeness. Rather, the treatise must be established as authoritative, which can be accomplished through the cross-examiner's own expert, or through judicial notice.

Additionally, because Rule 803(18) permits statements in learned treatises to be read in as evidence in chief, it avoids the unreality of admitting evidence for the purpose of impeachment only, with an instruction to the jury not to consider it otherwise. *See* Advisory Committee's note to rule 803(18), 56 F.R.D. 183, 316-17.

VI. REFUSAL TO RECOGNIZE LEARNED TREATISES

Typically, an expert or defendant doctor will attempt to frustrate cross-examination by refusing to acknowledge the authoritativeness of treatises. This can be especially acute when the cross-examiner has only one or two authorities upon which he was going to rely. There are several well-recognized tactics for dealing with this problem.

A. Overcoming Expert's Refusal in State Court

First, if the cross-examiner is aware of several authorities which support his position, he can pile them up on the counsel table, and then, one at a time, examine the doctor on whether he recognizes each work's or author's authoritativeness. With each work, the witness should be reminded of the author's credentials, or that the book is in its umpteenth printing, or that it is the textbook used in the expert's own medical school. The expert's continuous refusal to acknowledge his awareness or the authoritativeness of any of the examiner's treatises will cause him to appear in the eyes of the jury as uninformed, uncooperative, evasive or unbelievable.

Second, even if the cross-examiner has only one or two sources upon which he is relying, merely going through the litany of the book's or author's qualifications will have the desired effect (i.e., "Doctor, the text I am referring to is in its 18th edition. Are you aware of that?"; "Doctor, you are aware that the author, Dr. X., is chairman of the Department of Orthopedics at Harvard Medical School?"; or "Doctor, are you aware that this pamphlet is published by the American College of Obstetrics and Gynecology, of which you are a Fellow?").

Third, the defendant can be asked, on his deposition, whether he relies on or recognizes a specified medical text as authoritative, although he cannot be asked to list all books on a particular subject which he regards as authoritative or used in medical school. *Ithier v. Solomon*, 399 N.Y.S.2d 450, 59 A.D.2d 935 (2d Dep't, 1977). The examiner should make a list of every authority on the particular subject—whether or not it agrees with his position—and then ask the witness whether he recognizes each.

Finally, the examiner can, prior to confronting the witness with a specific book, establish that his medical knowledge is based not only upon his experience, but also derived in large part from lectures he has attended and from studies, journal articles, and authoritative texts and treatises he has read. His subsequent refusal to agree to the authoritativeness of any books, in light of this admission, will make the doctor look especially foolish.

B. Rule in Federal Court

The expert's tactic of refusing to recognize texts as authoritative does not apply in the Federal Courts. The attorney has the opportunity in Federal Court to depose the nonparty expert prior to trial. This should always be done and the attorney should establish at this deposition which treatises the expert recognizes. If the attorney determines in advance that the expert will not recognize the treatises in question, he can then have his own expert establish the authoritativeness of the sources on his direct case.

VII. ADVERSE PARTY RULE

In New York, it is very common for plaintiffs' attorneys to call the defendant doctor on his direct case as his first witness. This practice can lead to two potential problems.

In Federal Court, if the defendant has, on deposition, refused to acknowledge the authority of plaintiff's sources, then plaintiff's counsel will have to place his own expert on the witness stand first for the sole purpose of establishing the authoritativeness of the treatises.

A. Use of Learned Treatises under Adverse Party Rule

In State Court, there is a view held by a small minority of trial judges that precludes the use of treatises as a cross-examination tool when the defendant doctor is being questioned on plaintiff's direct case. *Ciaccio v. Housman, supra*. Under the adverse party rule, when the defendant doctor is called as a witness by plaintiff's counsel, it will be assumed that he is a hostile witness. Therefore, counsel can ask leading questions and the direct examination can, under the Court's supervision, assume the nature of cross-examination. *Becker v. Koch*, 104 N.Y. 394, 10 N.E 701 (1887); *Wolper v. New York Water Service Corporation*, 96 N.Y.S.2d 647, 276 A.D. 1106 (2d Dep't, 1950); *Gonzalez v. Medina*, 417 N.Y.S.2d 953, 69 A.D.2d 14 (1st Dep't, 1979). *McDermott v. Manhattan Eye, Ear, Nose and Throat Hospital*, 255 N.Y.S.2d 65, 15 N.Y.2d 20 203 N.E.2d 469 (1964), established the rule that a plaintiff in a medical malpractice action may call the defendant physician as a witness and examine him both as to his factual knowledge, and if he is qualified, as an expert to establish the generally accepted medical practice in the community. *See also Segrett v. Putnam Community Hospital*, 449 N.Y.S.2d 785, 88 A.D.2d 590 (2d Dep't, 1982); *Johnson v. New York City Health & Hospitals Corp.*, 374 N.Y.S.2d 343, 49 A.D.2d 234 (2d Dep't, 1975).

The majority of plaintiffs' attorneys and trial judges have, therefore, proceeded under the proposition that a full and complete cross-examination is permitted, and that a defendant doctor can be confronted with passages from concededly authoritative learned treatises which contradict his opinion, and be thus impeached. This view would seem to be a logical extension of the rules stated by the Court of Appeals in *Becker* and *McDermott, supra*. It would seem absurd to permit plaintiff's counsel, under the adverse witness rule, to lead the witness, cross-examine the witness, ask him for his expert opinion, impeach him with his own prior inconsistent statements (including texts which he has written and which contradict his testimony on the witness stand), but prevent him from impeaching the doctor with learned treatises.

B. Minority View

The trial court in *Ciaccio v. Housman*, *supra*, concluded, contrary to above analysis, that plaintiff's counsel cannot impeach a defendant doctor with learned treatises. As previously stated, the New York rule is that medical treatises are not admissible as substantive evidence, but can be used for impeachment purposes only. While the adverse party rule allows the "direct" examination of a defendant doctor to assume the nature of cross-examination, it has long been held that a party cannot impeach the credibility of a witness he calls. *Richardson on Evidence*, secs. 508, 520. The only exception to this rule allows such a witness to be impeached with his own prior inconsistent statements. CPLR sec. 4514. Following this logic, the defendant doctor can be impeached with prior inconsistent statements contained in his own writings,* but he cannot be impeached with contradictory statements contained in the writings of others. Since plaintiff's counsel cannot impeach a witness he calls by reading from authoritative sources that contradict the witness' opinion, then allowing plaintiff to read the contradictory passages has the effect of admitting them as direct evidence. "Plaintiff's attorney cannot do by indirection what he is prohibited from doing directly, that is, to use a medical text to show a departure from accepted practice by the defendant physician." *Ciaccio v. Housman*, *supra*, 411 N.Y.S.2d at 526.

The Court in *Ciaccio* conceded, however, that the plaintiff would not be "bound" by defendant's answers on "direct" and that while he may not impeach the witness by confronting him with contradictory opinions in treatises, he can contradict defendant's testimony by other evidence in the case. *Ciaccio v. Housman*, *supra*, 411 N.Y.S.2d at 525, citing *Becker v. Koch*, *supra*; *Spampinato v. ABC Construction Corp.*, 360 N.Y.S.2d 878, 880, 319 N.E.2d 196, 198 (1974); *Title Guarantee and Trust Co. v. Pam*, 232 N.Y. 441, 134 N.E. 525 (1922).

**See also McDermott v. Manhattan Eye, Ear, Nose and Throat Hospital*, *supra*, 255 N.Y.S.2d at 72. "In this case, the plaintiff insists that she hoped to prove by the testimony of Dr. Paton himself that he was guilty of malpractice—by questioning him as to the propriety of a corneal transplant in view of the condition of her eyes and, then, if necessary, by attempting to induce him to give testimony favorable to her case by use of his authoritative text on the subject. . . We perceive nothing wrong in such a technique or tactic, no any reason for denying the plaintiff the opportunity so to proceed."

VIII. PREPARATION OF EXPERTS

The effectiveness of cross-examination through the use of learned treatises underlines the need for the attorney to thoroughly prepare his own experts on the literature. The attorney must identify all articles, books and treatises which deal with the medical subject matter of the lawsuit, and prepare the expert physician to differentiate, distinguish or disagree with statements, contained in sources which he considers authoritative, which apparently contradict his own opinions.

Learned treatises can be a powerful tool for the cross-examination and impeachment of witnesses. An attorney thoroughly familiar with the medical literature can effectively balance the expert's natural advantage and go far in causing the jury to question the doctor's expertise or intellectual honesty.

CHAPTER TWENTY

PLAINTIFF'S REQUESTS TO CHARGE

Herman Schmertz, Esq.

I. DRAFTING REQUESTS FOR INSTRUCTIONS—OVERVIEW

A critical adjunct to timely and complete exceptions to legally erroneous or unfairly stressed instructions by the trial court, whether *sua sponte* or at the request of the defense, is the advance preparation—in writing—of counsel's own requcsts to charge. They should be carefully drafted, with supporting citations, to cover all critical areas of law and fact, as well as styled in a way which will best serve the client—yet always within—or better, *just within*—the bounds of legal correctness. There is a delicate balance situation involved here, which can be successfully met only through a time-consuming process, with meticulous attention to details. Requests for instructions, moreover, should never be limited to counsel's own primary contentions, but should include as well defensive requests, designed to blunt the effects of likely submissions from the opposition or certain traditional worrisome propositions which the court might charge on its own, owing to the particular type of case. Such defensive requests, in many instances, could be held back, until and if the occasion arises for submission.

It is often the fact that the only meritorious basis for an appeal will lie in the refusal of the court to charge in accordance with properly prepared and submitted requests. In general, then, a comprehensive submission is to be encouraged, guided always by good sense under all of the circumstances of a given case.

II. TYPES OF INSTRUCTIONS IN THE MALPRACTICE CASE

Following are illustrative examples of primary and defensive requests, in the malpractice case, to demonstrate that far more is involved than merely offering up to the court a computer-like series of well-known, abstract, legal principles.

A. Factual Contentions

There are quite advantageous ways—from the standpoint of jury appeal—of stating the ultimate fact issue. In a diagnostic malpractice case, for example, the attorney's use of language should produce something far beyond merely: "Plaintiff asserts that defendant did not properly diagnose his condition," to which the court will invariably add, *sua sponte*: "Defendant says he did," or "Defendant says he could not fairly be expected to uncover plaintiff's latent condition." Thus, the sort of embellishment along the lines of the suggestions below, employing repetition of key concepts in different words, might serve to clearly impress on the jurors' minds the gravity and scope of the cause of action:

> Plaintiff claims in this case that defendant physician was medically careless and negligent under the circumstances revealed and shown by the proof, for his failure to fulfill his obligation to adequately diagnose, through omission of proper testing, decedent's cardiac condition and thereby take such other measures as would have been required to enable his patient to survive and live out a normal life.
>
> Plaintiff claims, in other words, that defendant was medically careless and negligent under all of the circumstances revealed and shown by the proof, for his neglect to perform certain required medical testing, given the patient's symptoms, so as to have made a definitive diagnosis of coronary artery disease and thereby permit and allow measures to be taken in time to have saved him from sudden and untimely death.
>
> Plaintiff claims that had the administration and application of sound cardiac diagnostic care been employed, defendant physician, with reasonable probability, would have diagnosed decedent's coronary artery disease and thereupon have imparted sound and sufficient medical advice and employed other medical steps so as to avoid the worsening of his condition and his ultimate death.
>
> If you find, from all of the evidence, that plaintiff has established defendant's departure from sound cardiac care substantially in the manner claimed, then defendant physician is liable and responsible for all of the damages you reasonably conclude in your deliberations proximately resulted from that departure from due medical care and treatment, to the surviving wife and children of the decedent.

B. Defendant Physician's Duty of Care Defined in Terms of the Specific Facts

Where, as above, the *gravamen* of the alleged malpractice is failure to properly diagnose the patient's condition, the basic precept of sound medical care may be presented in terms which will best impart to the panel its crucial importance, yet remain within the bounds of legal propriety, preventing reversal if charged. Something on the following order could be considered:

> The legal obligation of defendant in the present case was to use and employ reasonable and competent medical skill in every aspect of his course of treatment of decedent. Defendant was required to employ reasonable medical skill and care in the diagnosis of the bodily condition of this patient. This included the taking and careful evaluation of medically necessary diagnostic procedures and tests reasonably required under the circumstances to furnish correct diagnosis. In other words, the physician's obligation begins with taking all reasonable and medically necessary steps, tests, measures and procedures designed to enable the physician to make the proper diagnosis of his patient's true condition.
>
> Not only must a physician practicing in the medical specialty of defendant take and apply all reasonable diagnostic procedures, but he must thereupon proceed further and apply reasonable medical skill and the application of his learning for the purpose of making a medically sound and accurate diagnosis of the actual nature of his patient's medical problem.
>
> A medically competent diagnosis is essential for proper care and treatment of the patient, so that, therefore, you are instructed that the defendant physician was obligated under the law applicable to this case to use due and reasonable medical care in diagnosing the nature of any infirmity or condition of decedent, so that treatment as medically required could be undertaken at a time and in a manner which would reasonably have been expected to save his life.

Or, let us suppose a case is based on failure to properly treat a concededly properly diagnosed condition. It is one thing to request merely that the doctor was required to treat plaintiff with due care, to which defendant will have the court add that the defense claim is that proper treatment was given. It is quite another to propose something in the order of the following, which will heighten the doctor's legal obligation, should take defense counsel by somewhat of a surprise, and render it quite difficult for him to respond meaningfully to it:

In the present case, defendant was obligated to attend his patient in compliance with proper accepted medical care in the treatment of a methadone overdosed patient. Where a physician undertakes to treat a patient for any adverse condition, including one caused or produced by ingestion of any drug prior to the time of the patient's arrival at the hospital, it is no defense to a claim of malpractice that the patient had ingested the drug in the first place or was allegedly careless in doing so. It was the physician's avowed task, which he fully accepted, to treat that condition with proper medical skill.

The law provides that conduct on the part of a patient prior to his arrival at a hospital for treatment must not be considered as contributory negligence, nor as any circumstance which relieves a hospital or a doctor from the full obligation of professional care in the treatment of that patient. The patient, under the law, has the right to rely on the professional commitment of responsible care and treatment, regardless of the source and origin of the patient's disorder, which legally binds the physician to the duty of rendering a proper course of treatment.

Therefore, in the present case, since plaintiff claims that defendant is liable by reason of his negligence in treating a patient suffering from the effects of a methadone overdose, you must not speculate as to any reason for the patient's having taken any drug in the first place nor place any responsibility upon him therefor. Irrespective of whether or not that conduct might or might not be considered unwise on his part, you must not consider it at all for the purpose of discharging defendant from liability or reducing his responsibility. The only relevance of decedent's taking of any drug prior to the time for his arrival at the hospital is to the issue of whether defendant was at fault in failing to treat him with proper medical care in the light of the condition from which he was suffering at that time.

C. Basic Medical Precepts

A grouping of requests should always contain these—of course—which are readily found, *as a starting point*, in a good treatise on jury instructions. But, by all means, never merely request that the court charge a particular page of a certain published work on pattern charges. Aside, very often, from certain dangerous qualifications which may be contained therein, they do not—quite frankly—do full justice to the proposition urged on the court in terms of your client's interest. Prepare the requests yourself; it makes a far better impression on the trial judge who may be more prone to accept them in that formal form, perhaps even slightly intimidated. Of equal importance, they may be easily marked as exhibits for appeal purposes if *any* are refused. Never adopt the precise words of any treatise, unless—in your case—the principle cannot be told for your client any better, within the limits of the law. Since that is quite rare, a general medical-legal precept should, where possible and useful, be expanded and presented so as to best suit your client's needs. The following is an illustration:

> A physician's obligation includes not only diagnosis and treatment, but also the giving of proper medical advice and instructions to his patient, including medical advice as to the patient's safe course of conduct. Whenever the principles of sound medical skill and care reasonably require, the physician is legally obligated to give all necessary advice and instructions to his patient as to the patient's following course of personal conduct, so as to prevent any and all risks of harm to the patient which reasonable medical care and skill in the giving of instructions would have avoided. I charge you that the failure on the part of defendant physician to satisfy his obligation of medical care with respect to any diagnostic measure or other medical precaution including medically necessary advice and instructions required for the proper care of his patient, requires a finding by you, the members of the jury, that the physician committed malpractice, so long as you also find that this was a proximate cause of the harm suffered, that is the death of decedent.

Suppose, for a further example, the physician is a youthful intern in the employ of defendant-hospital, who is apt to engender the compassion of the panel. His basic duty can be defined in a style which can go far in alleviating that ever-present hazard:

> A medical intern is held by the law, and I so instruct you, to the same standard of care as any other physician. Intern status does not change, diminish, decrease or lessen, to any extent, a physician's duty of care and constitutes no excuse or defense for acts or omissions constituting malpractice or medical negligence. In the eyes of the law, the intern status of a doctor does not by any means free him or relieve him from the obligation to use and exercise proper medical care in accordance

with good and sound medical practice. An intern is a physician, first and foremost, and he is chargeable by the law with the duty of exercising sound medical care in every medical connection with his patient. He is required to properly exercise his calling as a doctor and is responsible for conducting himself as a reasonably prudent doctor under the same circumstances.

D. The Defensive Request

The physician will almost invariably plead that he exercised his best judgment and, invariably, the court will charge standard legal doctrine to the effect that the physician is not liable merely for an error in judgment. While this is legally accurate in most cases, it is fraught with great peril. So it is imperative that something of this order be kept in readiness:

> Where medical malpractice is claimed, the fact that a physician might offer an alleged defense that he exercised his own best judgment in the care and treatment of his patient, or that he may have committed merely an error of judgment, will not constitute a legal excuse or defense to a cause of action predicated on medical negligence or malpractice, so long as the evidence indicates that the course of treatment or the methods and procedures utilized did not have reputable support in the profession, or violated that degree of skill and care which is a physician's duty to apply at all times.
>
> Despite a defendant physician's claim that he may have erred in judgment, he is still liable and responsible under the law if the judgment he made was not based on the intelligence, professional skill and ability which he was required to possess as a medical doctor.

Or, let us say that contributory negligence is asserted in mitigation of damages, because of the patient's alleged culpable conduct following administration of the medical care claimed to be professionally negligent. The plaintiff cannot simply rely on a general instruction which only admonishes the jury, in conclusory form, to free him from blame if he acted carefully. The attorney must elaborate on this theme in a manner which best assures that the panel will ultimately discount the culpable conduct defense. Here is an example:

In an action such as this to recover damages for the wrongful death of the decedent, plaintiff has no burden of proof as to whether decedent was free of contributory negligence. Defendant has the burden of proving by a preponderance of the evidence, that the decedent was guilty of contributory negligence which constituted a proximate cause of his death, that is a substantial factor in producing such death. If defendant fails to sustain that burden of proof by a preponderance of the evidence or if the evidence on the issue of contributory negligence is so evenly balanced that you cannot conclude that there is a preponderance on either side, you must find that the decedent was not negligent and not responsible in any way for his death.

In order for defendant to meet and comply with his burden of proof on his claim of contributory negligence on the part of decedent, defendant must establish each of the following by a preponderance of the evidence:

First, he must, of course, prove that decedent actually ingested valium after he was taken from the hospital.

Second, he must also establish that the valium which decedent is claimed to have taken after he left the hospital was a substantial factor in causing and producing his death, that is, that the valium taken after he left the hospital actually caused his death in whole or in part.

Third, defendant must additionally prove that the valium taken subsequent to decedent's removal from the hospital was not consumed or ingested as a direct result of any adverse physical or mental effects of any drugs still within him and administered to him while under defendant's care to alleviate his original condition.

Fourth, defendant must further prove that whether or not decedent was suffering from the physical or mental effects of the methadone at the time he is claimed to have taken valium, decedent was careless and negligent in taking valium, considering all of the circumstances as you find them to have existed. If he did not act unreasonably under those precise circumstances, then he cannot be considered negligent under any circumstances.

Therefore, defendant, to establish his burden of proof, must satisfy you by a preponderance of the evidence as to the existence of each and every one of the elements which the court has just stated. Any failure by defendant to establish any element by a fair preponderance of the evidence must result in a finding that decedent was not guilty of any contributory negligence which caused or contributed to his death.

III. CONCLUSION

Requests to charge—in conclusion—are spawned by counsel's creativity and diligence. It is definitely the obligation of the trial lawyer to devote time and attention to this far-too-often-overlooked task. It is a crucial responsibility for so many reasons and its value cannot be overstated.

CHAPTER TWENTY-ONE

DEFENDANT'S REQUESTS TO CHARGE

Robert Devine, Esq.

I. GENERAL CONSIDERATIONS

It is in the interest of both the plaintiff and the defendant to have the jury give an accurate verdict based upon clearly stated legal principles that frame the particular factual issues in controversy. From the plaintiff's point of view, where a general verdict is rendered and several theories of liability have been submitted to them, that verdict can stand only if *all* the theories submitted are sustained by the evidence. *Davis v. Caldwell*, 54 N.Y.2d 176, 178; *O'Boyle v. Avis Rent-A-Car System*, 78 A.D.2d 431, 437-438; *Kileen v. Reinhardt*, 71 A.D.2d 851, 853. From the defendant's point of view, there is little chance of reversal in the event of an adverse verdict, where the standard Pattern Jury Instruction Charge is given without specific principles applicable to the facts of the case on trial being requested.

A. Special Interrogatories

This can be handled in two ways. The first involves the use of Special Interrogatories, which is considered preferable by the Appellate Courts. *See Forman v. Davidson*, 74 A.D.2d 505 (1st Dep't 1980). In *Brant Corp. v. Warren Automatic Controls Corp.*, 37 A.D.2d 563 (2d Dep't 1971), the court stated: "We call attention to the trial bench that it would be well advised to make use of the procedures available for special verdict or a general verdict accompanied by written answers to interrogatories." *Zack Metal Co. v. Federal Ins. Co.*, 28 A.D.2d 1109, 284 N.Y.S.2d 582 (1st Dep't 1967) (citing CPLR sec. 4111).

This device is useful in a particular case where an attorney feels it would not be in the best interest of his client for the court to give the jury an exposition of the law. As is pointed out in *New York Civil Practice* by Weinstein-Korn-Miller, sec. 4111.03 p. 41-187, 188, "Since the court applies the law to the facts found by the jury, the special verdict obviates the need for charging the jury concerning legal principles and the possibility of error accordingly is reduced." It must be noted, however, that it rests within the discretion of the court to decide whether to use these interrogatories. CPLR sec. 4111; *Johnson v. Arthraft Strauss Sign Corp.*, 45 A.D.2d 482 (1974). Thus, failure to use interrogatories may not be a ground for reversal unless there was an abuse of discretion. *Quigley v. County of Suffolk*, 75 A.D.2d 888 (2d Dep't 1980).

B. *Green v. Downs* Criteria

The other way of having the jury identify the issues that they must decide is insuring that the court follows the dictates of the Court of Appeals as set forth in *Green v. Downs*, 27 N.Y.2d 205, 316 N.Y.S.2d 221 (1970). This requires that the court state and outline the disputed issues of fact as the nature of the case and the evidence may require; set forth specific, rather than abstract principles of law; and relate these principles to the facts of the case. *See Zipoy v. Benson*, 47 A.D.2d 233, 235 (1975).

It is advisable, therefore, for any defendant's attorney to submit to the court, in writing, not only "Requests to Charge," but also "Defendant's Contentions." This should be done in a fair manner with each contention supported by competent evidence in the record. For example:

DEFENDANT'S CONTENTIONS

Defendant physician contends that he conformed to good and accepted practice in prescribing and administering the drug ______________________________. He contends that the reaction that the plaintiff suffered was due, not to malpractice on his part, but to an unusual allergic reaction that could not have been either foreseen or prevented. He contends, through his attorney, that although he did not inform this patient of the risk of this reaction, a reasonably prudent person in the plaintiff's position would have decided to take this drug, if fully informed. Finally, he contends that the plaintiff's complaints today, if true, are due to the underlying disease for which he treated her, rather than from the reaction caused by the medication.

Obviously, there will be standard Requests to Charge that can be used by a defendant in almost every malpractice case. For example:

1: I CHARGE YOU that the fact that a complication occurred following medical treatment does not give rise to an inference of negligence or malpractice on the part of the defendant physician.

De Falco v. Long Island College Hospital, 90 Misc. 2d 164, *aff'd*, 62 A.D.2d 1180.

-or-

2: I CHARGE YOU that the defendant physician is to be judged on the facts as they existed at the time and not in retrospect, and in light of subsequent events.

Henry v. Bronx Lebanon Medical Center, 53 A.D.2d 476, 385 N.Y.S.2d 772, 69 A.L.R.2d 1250.

But, in addition, a Request to Charge a general principle, should be linked to a Request to Charge that principle as applied to the facts of the case. For example:

3: I CHARGE YOU that a physician is entitled to make a judgment in determining what course of treatment he will render. In doing so he has the right to balance the risks and advantages of each form of treatment. He cannot be held liable for such a judgment decision.

Topel v. Long Island Jewish Medical Center, 76 A.D.2d 862, 428 N.Y.S.2d 507, *aff'd*, 55 N.Y.2d 682, 446 N.Y.S.2d 932 (1981).

4: I CHARGE YOU, in this connection, under the evidence in this case, the decision to give antibiotics or not was a judgment decision, for which there can be no liability.

II. PARTICULAR CONSIDERATIONS

Requests to Charge should be given to the Trial Judge long enough in advance so that he or his secretary can incorporate them in his Charge. Psychologically, where the work has already been done for him, the Judge will be more inclined to use your wording than when he fully prepares his Charge and then you ask for additional items. Of course, since you will probably be asked to exchange requests with your adversary, you should not hand in your Requests too far in advance, since they could telegraph your defense. Since the plaintiff's case will probably be over and you know his approach anyway, you could lose something in a premature exchange.

The written Requests should be marked for identification as a Court Exhibit so they become part of the Record on Appeal. Exceptions to the failure of the Judge to Charge specific Requests should be made on the Record before the jury retires or else they are waived. CPLR sec. 5501(a)(3). In fact, it would be wise to make your position known, on the Record, in the Presummation Conference, CPLR sec. 4110(b), so that the Judge has a better opportunity to adopt your requests.

III. CONCLUSION

Requests to Charge are a key part in the defense of a malpractice case. They aid a jury in focusing in on the issues which they must resolve. Jurors are extremely attentive to the Judge's instructions, since up to that stage of the trial they have heard nothing but a partisan approach from both sides. A case can be won or lost by a careful preparation of Requests. Moreover, if the Record is fully protected, and a valid Charge is not given, a defendant's lawyer can get two bites of the apple, i.e, a chance at a jury verdict initially, or, a reversal in the event of an adverse verdict. It certainly makes it easier, waiting for a jury verdict, with this in mind. To that extent alone, Requests to Charge are invaluable.

CHAPTER TWENTY-TWO

RECENT DEVELOPMENTS IN THE LAW OF MEDICAL MALPRACTICE: SUMMARY

Honorable Fred T. Santucci

THE 1985 MEDICAL MALPRACTICE LAW

In its second major attempt within the last decade, the New York State Legislature has sought "to reduce the escalating cost of Malpractice Insurance and to improve the adjudication of Malpractice claims . . . in order to insure the continued availability and affordability of quality health care services in this State."

The multi-pronged approach, effective July 1, 1985, amends the CPLR, Education Law, Insurance Law and Judiciary Law.

The legislation places greater responsibility upon hospitals to police their medical and support staff. It limits and "structures" the payment of damage awards and reduces attorneys' fees. The amendments expedite court intervention, liberalize pretrial discovery, and mandate that there be extended insurance coverage made available for those physicians and dentists who seek it.

The following is offered to assist the practitioner in dealing with medical and dental malpractice cases under the new law. However, one should be aware that many rules and regulations have yet to be promulgated by various governmental agencies.

I. HOSPITALS—PHYSICIANS—DENTISTS

A new section 2805-J of the Public Health Law requires every hospital to maintain and coordinate a program for the identification and prevention of medical and dental malpractice. A "Quality Assurance Committee" shall be established to oversee the facility's malpractice program, to monitor each incident and assure that the information gathered is utilized to "review and revise hospital procedures." The statute requires periodic review of the performance of those physicians enjoying hospital privileges and of all persons employed or associated with the hospital, and provides for privilege sanction procedures. The hospital is required to keep records as to "negative health care outcomes, incidents injurious to patients, patient grievances, professional liability premiums, settlements, awards and costs incurred by the hospital for patient injury prevention and safcty improvement activities."

Information gathered in the above-mentioned way is to be maintained in the individual physician's or dentist's personnel and credential file and is to be made available to other institutions to which a physician or dentist may apply for privileges.

The statute requires that hospitals provide a "procedure for the prompt resolution of grievances . . . that may result in claims for Medical or Dental Malpractice." Public Health Law sec. 2805-J(d). The Commissioner of Health is required to promulgate regulations to effectuate the procedure.

The disciplining of individual physicians is enlarged pursuant to Education Law, new section 6509(d).

The legislation provides additional funding for the Office of Professional Medical Conduct through increased registration fees and a $2,000,000 appropriation from the State Budget.

Revision of the Insurance Law mandates that medical malpractice insurance premiums be based upon a physician's record with respect to incidents of alleged malpractice and upon any other factors deemed relevant by the Superintendant of Insurance. Ins. Law secs. 2343(d). Physicians and dentists who maintain insurance coverage in the amount of $1,000,000 per claimant and $3,000,000 aggregate may request and must be granted additional coverage of $1,000,000 and $3,000,000, either from their insurers or, if they from time to time provide emergency medical care in a hospital at which they have privileges, from said hospital. *See* Ins. Law secs. 2343(d), 3437.

II. IN THE COURTHOUSE: PRETRIAL DISCOVERY

For all actions, regardless of their nature, commenced on or after July 1, 1985, pretrial discovery has been liberalized by the revision of CPLR sec. 3101(d), which provides for discoverability of expert opinion or other material prepared for litigation. Upon request, each party shall disclose the identity, qualifications, and the subject of the expert's expected testimony including the grounds for his or her opinion. If a party can show that it retained the expert just prior to trial, the expert's testimony shall not be precluded solely for noncompliance with the new Rule. However, in dental or medical malpractice cases, the parties may omit the names of dental or medical experts. If, pursuant to CPLR sec. 3101(a)(3), a party wishes to take his own retained or treating expert physician's or dentist's examination before trial, the other parties shall have full disclosure with respect to that expert without court order. CPLR sec. 3101(d)(1)(ii).

The revision of CPLR sec. 3101 also permits the discovery of materials prepared for litigation upon a showing of a substantial need for the material and an inability to obtain it by other means without undue hardship. Disclosure of mental impressions, conclusions, and opinions of legal theories remain protected.

III. CALENDAR PRACTICE

New CPLR Rule 3406 requires that in medical or dental malpractice actions commenced on or after July 1, 1985, a notice be filed with the clerk of the court within sixty days after Joinder of Issue with proof of service upon all other parties. The time for filing may be extended only upon motion pursuant to CPLR sec. 2004. The notice shall contain proof of compliance with demands for authorizations for medical, dental or hospital records.

The new section requires that after Joinder of Issue a pre-calendar conference be held that shall include settlement discussions, the establishment of a timetable for pretrial disclosure and trial. All disclosure must be completed within twelve months of the filing of the notice and the parties must be ready for trial no later than eighteen months after the filing of the original notice. The section provides for the imposition of sanctions that may include dismissal or the granting of judgment by default, for failure to comply with the calendar control rules set forth.

IV. MEDICAL MALPRACTICE PANELS

The Medical Malpractice Panel continues under Judiciary Law sec. 148-a. However, Suffolk County and the Fifth Judicial District are exempted from the Panel requirements and the Chief Administrator of the courts is to conduct a study of the impact of this exemption via comparison of the rate of disposition between the exempted districts and the Seventh Judicial District and Nassau County.

V. DAMAGES

CPLR Rule 4111(d) and Rule 4213(b), which require the itemization of damages by the trier of fact as to special and general damages in a medical malpractice case, have been extended to dental malpractice actions. In addition, it is now required that damages shall be itemized as to those incurred before the verdict and those to be incurred in the future. The trier of fact shall "set forth the period of years ovcr which such amounts are intended to provide compensation and shall make the full award of future damages without reduction to present value."

CPLR sec. 4545(a) (commonly known as the Collateral Source Rule, under which the verdict is reduced by the amount of compensation received by the plaintiff through independent sources) has been amended to include actions in dental malpractice. The scope of this Rule has been broadened to include payment of future costs or expenses that the court may find will with reasonable certainty be replaced or indemnified, less the projected future costs of maintaining the benefits.

VI. PERIODIC PAYMENTS—CPLR ARTICLE 50

As to actions sounding in medical and dental malpractice commenced on or after July 1, 1985, the new statute provides in essence that all awards attributable to future damages in excess of $250,000 must be paid to the plaintiff in installments or periodic payments. That portion of any award for future damages in excess of $250,000 attributable to pain and suffering must be paid in installments not to exceed ten years. Should the trier of fact determine that pain and suffering shall not endure for ten years, but for a lesser period of time, the payments shall be made over that lesser period. The statute further requires that the court calculate the cost of an annuity and to enter judgment in the amount of the present value of the annuity contract required to make the payments. The statute requires that the defendants and their insurance carriers offer and guarantee the purchase and payment of the required annuity contract. Payments pursuant to the contract shall be increased annually by 4 percent. The annuity contract must be issued by qualified insurers approved by the Superintendent of Insurance and by the court. CPLR sec. 5039. CPLR sec. 5033 sets forth security posting requirements to be met by defendants and insurers to guarantee the periodic payments and provides measures by which the requirements of this section may be enforced by plaintiffs and codefendants. One such measure provides for entry of judgment against a defaulting defendant in a lump sum as such sum is determined under law without regard to Article 50.

Pursuant to CPLR sec. 5034, if the defendant for any reason fails to make a payment as required by Article 50, the plaintiff may seek a court order requiring the lump sum payment by the defaulting party of all outstanding installments, which sum shall not be discounted to present value.

If the plaintiff should die before payments are completed, liability for payments due for medical, dental and other health costs or non-economic loss not yet due at the time of the plaintiff's death is terminated. CPLR sec. 5035. Periodic payments due for loss of future earnings shall not be reduced or terminated by the death of the plaintiff, but shall continue to be paid to those to whom the plaintiff owed a duty of support at the time of his or her death, until that duty ceases or until the end of the period of payment originally found by the jury, whichever occurs first. Where the plaintiff owes no duty of support, or where the duty subsequently ceases, the legislation recognizes the right of expectancy of inheritance by providing that the periodic payments shall be a part of the deceased plaintiff's estate. To assist in the early settlement of estates, CPLR sec. 5035(b) provides that upon motion by an interested party the court may convert the remaining payments to a lump sum by calculating the present value.

Pursuant to CPLR sec. 5036, in cases of hardship, the court may order payment of the remaining payments or a portion thereof in a lump sum based upon the present value of the payments remaining, due to unanticipated medical, dental, or other expenses, if such payment would not unreasonably burden the defendants and if the interests of justice would be furthered.

Periodic payments under CPLR Article 50 may be assignable under certain conditions to secure alimony payments, maintenance, child support, attorneys' fees and expenses of litigation and for the costs of products, services and accomodations for medical, dental, or other health care.

VII. SETTLEMENTS

Settlement agreements reached by the parties are not subject to the provisions of the new Article and accordingly, it is not required that they be structured. CPLR sec. 5037.

VIII. FRIVOLOUS CLAIMS

New section 8303 of the CPLR provides for the awarding of costs and attorneys' fees up to the amount of $10,000 against a party who brings and/or maintains a frivolous claim, counterclaim, cross claim or defense if it was " . . . commenced, used or continued in bad faith, solely to delay or prolong the resolution of the litigation, or to harass, or maliciously injure another," or if it was ". . . commenced or continued in bad faith without any basis in law or fact and could not be supported by a good faith argument for an extension, modification or reversal of existing law."

IX. ATTORNEYS' FEES

Judiciary Law sec. 474(a) has been revised and broadened in scope to cover all retainers executed on or after July 1, 1985, in dental as well as medical malpractice matters.

The sliding scale for allowable contingent fees has been revised downward to provide for 30 percent of the first $250,000 recovered, 25 percent of the next $250,000 recovered, 20 percent of the next $500,000 recovered, 15 percent of the next $250,000 recovered and 10 percent of any amount over $1,250,000 recovered. The right of an attorney, in good faith, to seek compensation over and above the sliding scale due to extraordinary circumstances has been preserved.

The 33⅓ percent contingency fee retainer is no longer available as an alternative in medical and dental malpractice matters.

Attorneys' fees are to be paid up front in a lump sum with the fee based upon the present value of the future periodic payments to be made pursuant to the new CPLR Article 50.

X. INDIVIDUAL ASSIGNMENT SYSTEM

Under the proposed new I.A.S. Rules most cases would not "trigger" the participation of the court until a motion is made or Note of Issue filed, at which time the court takes control of a case. However, in medical and dental malpractice cases, the filing of a notice within sixty days after issue is joined, CPLR sec. 3406 brings a matter before the court for early conferencing, limiting of issues, scheduling of discovery and a panel hearing (if necessary). It should be noted that under Uniform Rule 202.3(c), which authorizes the Chief Administrator to establish special categories of cases for assignment to designated judges, it would be feasible to create a special part for medical and dental malpractices cases. Such part might be presided over by one judge, who would receive the cases upon the filing of the notices, and handle all conferences, discovery matters, motions and panel hearings (where required). Upon completion of a panel hearing, a matter would be assigned to an I.A.S. Part for trial. This would ensure consistency and eliminate duplicative efforts in conferencing and motion practice.

If more than one judge could be assigned to preside over the special malpractice part, a case could remain in such part for trial before the non-panel judge, in conformity with Judiciary Law sec. 148-a(4).

However, if no special part is established for malpractice cases, such matters will be assigned to a judge sitting in an I.A.S. Part for conferencing, scheduling of discovery, and motion practice. Within one year of the filing of the Notice, after the completion of discovery and the filing of a Statement of Readiness, each matter shall be assigned to a Medical Malpractice Panel Part where a panel shall be convened pursuant to Judiciary Law sec. 148-a (except in Suffolk County and the Fifth Judicial District).

After the panel hearing, if no disposition is reached within thirty days, the matter will be re-assigned for trial to the original I.A.S. Part from whence it came.

In summary, the seven steps to be taken under the revised statutes and uniform Rules in medical or dental malpractices cases are as follows:

1. Sixty days after Joinder of Issue, Notice must be filed with the court. This section also sets forth the form of the notice.

2. Within sixty days after filing of the notice, the matter is to be conferenced by the court.

3. Within twelve months after the filing of the notice, all discovery must be completed.

4. Upon completion of discovery, a Certificate of Readiness must be filed.

5. Within thirty days of the filing of the Certificate of Readiness, or at such time as directed by the court, Medical Malpractice Panel contention papers must be submitted. (Except in Suffolk County and the Fifth Judicial District.)

6. A Medical Malpractice Panel is to be convened and a hearing held where required.

7. Within thirty days after the panel hearing and no later than eighteen months after the filing of the original Notice under Step 1, a Note of Issue must be filed and the parties must be ready for trial.

The panel requirements set forth in Steps 5, 6 and 7 are not applicable to dental malpractice cases.

XI. CONCLUSION

With the enactment of the new "Medical and Dental Malpractice Bill," the Legislature has made significant statutory changes in the law of our state. Although the bill's passage will have immediate impact upon the health care recipient, as well as upon the practice of medicine, dentistry and law, its full effect will not be known for a considerable time. Review and revision will no doubt be required to carry out the purposes envisioned by the drafters of the legislation.

TABLE OF AUTHORITIES

CASES

STATUTES

Federal Statutes

New York State Statutes

INDEX

ABOUT THE AUTHORS

EMMETT AGOGLIA, ESQ.

Mr. Agoglia is a partner of the firm McCoy & Agoglia, P.C., in Mineola, New York. He received his law degree from St. John's in 1958. His primary area of practice is in personal injury litigation. Mr. Agoglia is a member of the American Trial Lawyers Association, the Nassau County Bar Association and is the chairman of the New York State Bar Association's Committee of Senior Volunteers. Mr. Agoglia's numerous publications include "Special Problems in Hospital Litigation," which was published in *Hospital in Litigation* (1978) by the Practicing Law Institute, "Utilization of Reference Materials in the Preparation of a Personal Injury Case," and "Plaintiff's View of a Products Liability Case," co-authored with Kathleen Beckett, which was published in *Prepare Personal Injury Cases for Trial* (1984).

KATHLEEN BECKETT, ESQ.

Ms. Beckett is a 1975 graduate of Fordham University. She is currently an associate with the firm of McCoy & Agoglia, P.C., in Mineola, New York. Ms. Beckett is a member of the New York State, American and Nassau County Bar Associations. Her P.L.I. articles include "Medical Malpractice" and "Proof of Damages in Personal Injury Actions" (with Emmett Agoglia).

RICHARD COBURN, M.D.

Dr. Coburn is a self-employed plastic surgeon practicing in New York City. He also received his law degree from Fordham University in 1984. Dr. Coburn is a member of the American Medical Association, the International Association of Dental Research, the Transplantation Society, the American College of Surgeons, the Massachusetts Medical Society, the New York State and County Medical Societies, the Pan American Medical Association and the American Society of Plastic and Reconstructive Surgeons. Dr. Coburn has received several academic appointments and has published extensively in the medical field.

IRA COHEN, ESQ.

Mr. Cohen received his J.D. degree from Indiana University in 1968. He is currently in private practice in New York City, with his primary areas of practice being medical malpractice and civil litigation. Since 1977 Mr. Cohen has been Seminar Director and Consultant for the New York Law Journal Seminars. The medical malpractice seminars he has participated in include the Northwestern University Medical Malpractice Seminar for Dentists, the Medical Malpractice Seminar for Physicians and the Wisconsin Medical Association Seminar on Medical Malpractice for Physicians.

JOSEPH M. COSTELLO, ESQ.

Mr. Costello is a senior partner with the New York City firm of Costello & Shea. A 1951 graduate of Fordham Law School, his primary areas of practice include: products liability, medical/professional malpractice claims and general negligence defense. Mr. Costello is the Chairman of the Executive Committee of the Trial Lawyers Section of the New York State

Bar Association. He is also a member of the American Bar Association, the American Board of Professional Liability Attorneys, the International Association of Insurance Counsel, the Medical Defense Lawyers Association, and the Federal Bar Council. Mr. Costello has written for the New York Law Journal and for the Defense Journal.

ROBERT DEVINE, ESQ.

Mr. Devine is a partner of the firm Ivone, Devine and Jensen in Lake Success, New York. He received his law degree from Georgetown in 1964. His primary area of practice is the defense of medial malpractice and negligence cases. Mr. Devine is a member of the Executive Committee of the Trial Lawyers Section of the New York State Bar Association, and Chairman of Continuing Legal Education for that section. He is also a member of Action Unit #6 of the Association. Mr. Devine has served as chairman of the seminar "Structured Settlements," co-chairman of "Products Liability" and a panelist on "The Art of Discovery."

PETER C. KOPFF, ESQ.

Mr. Kopff is a partner in the New York City firm of Kopff, Nardelli & Dopf. His primary area of practice is the defense of medical malpractice litigation. He is a 1975 graduate of Albany Law School. Mr. Kopff is currently a member of the Trial Lawyers Section of the New York State Bar Association, the Association of the Bar of the City of New York, the American Bar Association, the New York County Lawyers Association, the Brooklyn-Manhattan Trial Counsel Association and the Defense Research Institute.

STANLEY A. LANDERS, ESQ.

Mr. Landers is a 1976 graduate of St. John's Law School and is currently practicing in New York City. His primary area of practice is plaintiff's medical malpractice. Mr. Landers is a member of the New York State Trial Lawyers Association, the American Trial Lawyers Association and the Queens County Bar Association.

HARRY H. LIPSIG, ESQ.

Admitted to the bar in 1926, Mr. Lipsig is a senior partner in the firm of Lipsig, Sullivan & Liapakis, P.C., in New York City. His primary area of practice is in general litigation. Mr. Lipsig is a member of the City of New York, Bronx, New York State, American and International Bar Associations. He is also a member of the Association of Trial Lawyers of America, the Brooklyn-Manhattan and Metropolitan Trial Lawyers Associations, the Women's Bar Associations of New York, Bronx, Brooklyn, Queens and Nassau. Among Mr. Lipsig's numerous publications are "Educational Malpractice Recovery Theories Needed," N.Y.L.J., Aug. 14, 1979 and "Forum Non Conveniens In Personal Injury Cases," N.Y.L.J. Feb. 28, 1979.

JOHN LOPRESTI, JR., ESQ.

Mr. LoPresti is a practicing attorney in New York City. He received his law degree from New York Law School in 1971. Mr. LoPresti is a former Appellate Division law clerk, working in Anthony L. Schlavetti's office. From September 1975 to June 1981, he was an adjunct professor at New York Law School. Mr. LoPresti is currently a member of the New York State and Richmond County bars.

JOHN R. MARSHALL, JR., ESQ.

Mr. Marshall is the Assistant Attorney General in charge of the Binghamton, New York Regional Office. He is a 1961 graduate of Syracuse University College of Law. His association memberships include the American, New York State, Chenango County and Broome County Bar Associations. Mr. Marshall is a member of the New York State Bar Automobile Association Traffic Safety Committee and the New York State Bar Association's Trial Lawyers Section, Continuing Legal Education Committee. He is the past president of the New York State Association of Towns and co-founder and second President of the New York State Association of Traffic Safety Boards.

STEVEN E. PEGALIS, ESQ.

Mr. Pegalis is a 1965 graduate of New York Law School. He is currently a partner in the Great Neck, New York, firm of Pegalis & Wachsman, P.C. Some of the organizations in which Mr. Pegalis is a member include: the American Trial Lawyers Association, the New York State Trial Lawyers Association, the American College of Medicine (Associate in Law), and the American Society of Law and Medicine. Mr. Pegalis is a member of the faculty of the Practicing Law Institute in the medical malpractice and trial practice area. He is a frequent lecturer in the area of medical malpractice for such organizations as the New York Law Journal Seminars Series and the New York State Bar Association. His numerous publications include the three volume set *American Law of Medical Malpractice*, published by Lawyers Cooperative Publishing Company.

LUKE H. PITTONI, ESQ.

Mr. Pittoni is the Vice President of Heidell, Pittoni & Moran, a New York City law firm. He is a 1971 graduate of Fordham Law School and his primary areas of practice are civil trials and appeals, medical malpractice, products liability and maritime. Mr. Pittoni is a member of numerous associations which include the American Board of Professional Liability Attorneys, the New York State Bar Association and the American Society of Law and Medicine. Mr. Pittoni has participated in P.L.I., Law Journal and American Bar Association seminars.

THOMAS J. PRINCIPE, ESQ.

Mr. Principe is a 1973 graduate of St. John's University Law School. He is presently an associate in the law firm of Morris & Duffy, located in New York City. His primary areas of practice are in insurance, negligence, medical malpractice and military law. Mr. Principe is defense council to the 42d Infantry Division, New York Army National Guard. The Associations in which he is a member include the New York State Bar Association, the Florida Bar Association and the Queens County Bar Association.

HON. FRED T. SANTUCCI

Justice Santucci was graduated from New York Law School in 1957 and was engaged in the general practice of the law until 1973, when he was elected to the Civil Court of the City of New York. During his tenure as a Judge of the Civil Court, Justice Santucci served as Coordinator of the Housing Part and as Co-Chairman of the court's Continuing Legal Education

Committee. Elected to the Supreme Court for the Eleventh Judicial District in 1978, Justice Santucci has presided over the Special Term for Medical Malpractice since 1980. His organizational memberships include the New York State and Queens County Bar Associations.

HERMAN SCHMERTZ, ESQ.

Mr. Schmertz is a partner in the firm of Gair, Gair & Conason in New York City. His primary area of practice is personal injury litigation. He received his law degree in 1960 from New York University. Mr. Schmertz is currently a member of the American Trial Lawyers Association, the New York State Trial Lawyers Association, the New York County Lawyers Association and the Bar Associations of Queens and Nassau. He has written for the Queens Bar Bulletin and was chief editor of the New York State Trial Lawyers Quarterly from 1980 to 1982.

ARTHUR N. SEIFF, ESQ.

Mr. Seiff is a practicing attorney in New York City with his primary interest in appellate practice. He is a 1924 graduate of New York University Law School and a member of the American and New York State Bar Associations and the Association of the Bar of the City of New York. Mr. Seiff was a former chairman on the Medical Jurisprudence Committee of the Association of the Bar of the City of New York and has previously written chapters on trial evidence and lectured for the Practicing Law Institute.

RICHARD E. SHANDELL, ESQ.

Mr. Shandell graduated from Columbia University School of Law in 1956. He is presently a member of the New York City firm of Glaser, Shandell & Blitz. Mr. Shandell is Governor of the Association of Trial Lawyers of America and past president of the New York State Trial Lawyers Association. He is a frequent lecturer for the New York State Trial Lawyers Association and for the Law Journal Seminar Press programs. He is the author of *The Preparation and Trial of Medical Malpractice Cases* by Law Journal Seminar Press.

H. R. SIMON, R. Ph., J.D.

Mr. Simon is a 1972 graduate of Washington College of Law of American University and is currently practicing with his firm in New York City. His primary areas of practice include medical malpractice, products liability and toxic torts. Mr. Simon is a member of numerous associations including the New York State Bar Association, the New York County Lawyers Association and the American Trial Lawyers Association. Mr. Simon has lectured at New York University Law School and Fordham University Law School and has participated in "Press in Medical Malpractice" and "Products Liability" seminars. Mr. Simon's publications include *Drug Products Liability* (1981) and he was a contributing author in *Cross Examination of Medical Experts* (1983).

HARVEY F. WACHSMAN, M.D., J.D., FCLM

Dr. Wachsman is a partner in the law firm of Pegalis & Wachsman, P.C., of Great Neck, New York, which concentrates its practice in the medical malpractice area. He is also a partner in the Newton, Connecticut firm of Wachsman & Wachsman. Dr. Wachsman received his medical degree in 1962, from Chicago Medical School. He received his J.D. degree from Brooklyn Law School, where he is an assistant adjunct professor of law. Dr. Wachsman's numerous fellowships include those with the American College of Legal Medicine, the American

Academy of Forensic Sciences and the Royal Society of Arts, London, England. Dr. Wachsman's lengthy list of publications include the three volume set *American Law of Medical Malpractice*, written with Steven Pegalis. He is also a frequent lecturer in the area of Medical Malpractice.

HARVEY WEITZ, ESQ.

Mr. Weitz is a partner in the firm of Schneider, Kleinick and Weitz, P.C., in New York City. He received his law degree in 1954 from Brooklyn Law School where he is now a visiting lecturer. Mr. Weitz's publications include: *Culpable Conduct: The New Law of Comparative Negligence*. He was Editor-in-Chief, from 1972-82, of Trial Lawyers Quarterly. Organizations in which he is a member include the New York State Bar Association, New York State Trial Lawyers Association and the Advisory Panel of the National Forensic Center.

ERNEST F. W. WILDERMUTH, JR., ESQ.

Mr. Wildermuth graduated from Brooklyn Law School in 1960 and is currently a partner in the firm of Montfort, Healy, McGuire & Salley, in Mineola, New York. His primary area of practice is tort claims. Mr. Wildermuth is a retired Lt. Col., in the New York Air National Guard. He is a member of the Nassau County, and Queens County Bar Associations. He is also a member of the Trial Lawyers Section of the New York State Bar Association.